Dear Mum
I saw this book and
thoft of you,
Merry christmas
Lots of love Lila

Dear mummy,
Ditoon lila!

( make lila have
mini mouse hair!
page 85)

# the VINTAGE TEA PARTY year

## Angel Adoree

MITCHELL BEAZLEY

To the magnificent people in my life that fill me with love, hope, support and inspiration. THANK YOU X

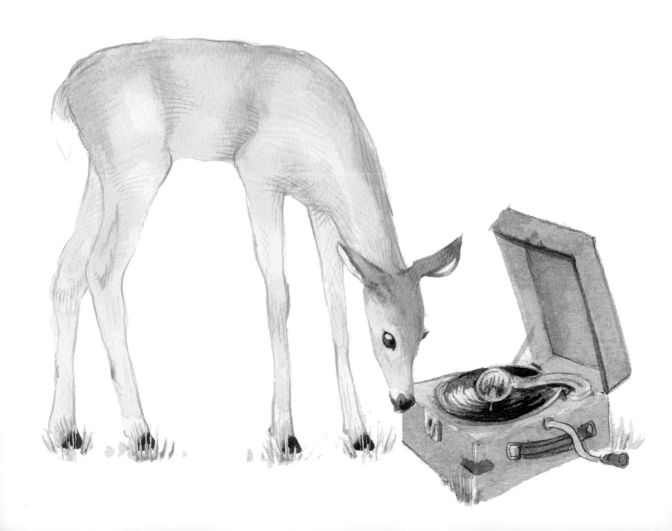

**The Vintage Tea Party Year**
by Angel Adoree

First published in Great Britain in 2012 by Mitchell Beazley,
an imprint of Octopus Publishing Group Limited,
Endeavour House, 189 Shaftesbury Avenue, London WC2H 8JY
www.octopusbooks.co.uk

An Hachette UK Company | www.hachette.co.uk

**Note** This book contains some dishes made with raw or lightly cooked eggs.
It is prudent for more vulnerable people such as pregnant and nursing mothers, invalids,
the elderly, babies and young children to avoid dishes made with uncooked or lightly cooked eggs.

**Commissioning Editor** Eleanor Maxfield | **Deputy Art Director & Designer** Yasia Williams-Leedham | **Senior Editor** Leanne Bryan | **Creative Director** Angel Adoree | **Photographers** Yuki Sugiura (food & drink); David Edwards (projects & locations) | **Illustrator** Adele Mildred | **Home Economist** Laura Fyfe | **Assistant Home Economist** Maura Cook | **Head of Craft** Sarah Keen | **Hair & Make-up** Sophia Hunt | **Copy Editor** Salima Hirani | **Proofreader** Jo Richardson | **Indexer** Isobel McLean | **Senior Production Controller** Caroline Alberti |

ISBN: 978 1 84533 725 4

A CIP catalogue record for this book is available from the British Library.

Set in Reminga, Gorey, Justlefthand and Lady Rene.

Printed and bound in China.

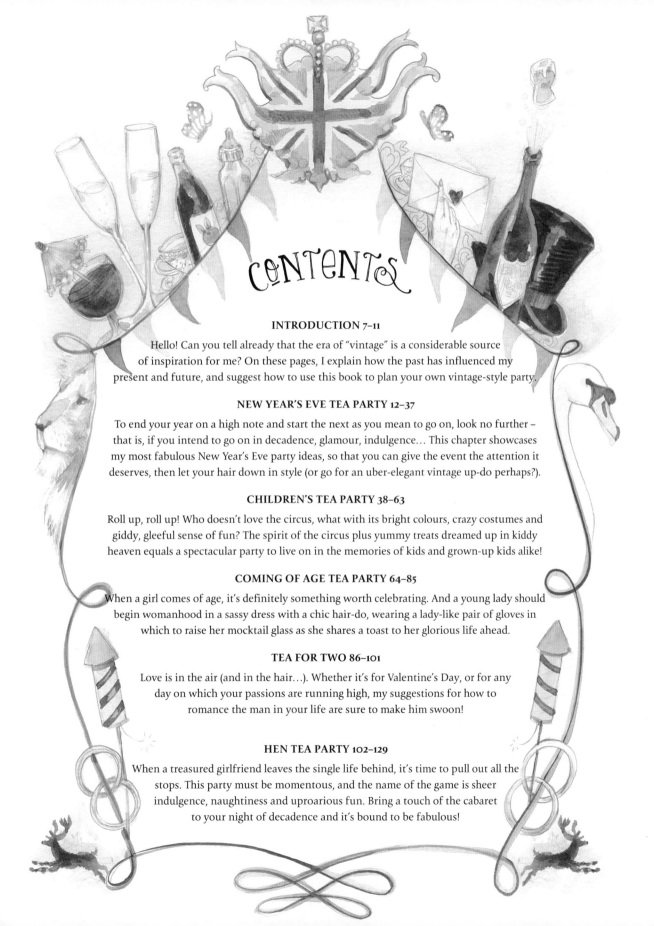

# CONTENTS

# INTRODUCTION

Welcome to *The Vintage Tea Party Year*. You are about to embark on a bespoke journey with me as I share and celebrate my passion for all things vintage. The following pages are inspired by the miracle of what Mother Nature has bestowed upon us through her four seasons, and I hope that they will, in turn, inspire your perfect tea party.

This book is divided into 12 chapters, which loosely represent a calendar year. I run a business that turns tea-party dreams into reality, offering people a little escapism from today's hectic life by transporting them to a time when life was simpler, yet steeped in glamour and decadence. I use the term "tea party" loosely – for me the phrase has evolved over the years into a style reference for the type of parties my company masterminds, rather than an afternoon treat taken between lunch and dinner, and the demand for vintage-style tea parties of all shapes and sizes is now bigger than ever. In fact, this book has been inspired by you! With a few expert tips, there's no reason why you can't do the same just as successfully. To organize the perfect vintage tea party, you must:

**1** Know your occasion – often they are chosen for us – wedding, hen party, Christmas. But there are times when you get to choose, too! Why not throw a tea party simply because you can?!

**2** Use this book to help you select the best foods, drinks and décor for your event – each of the 12 chapters is based on a specific type of occasion. Use the appropriate chapter for inspiration, but there's no need to stick religiously to ideas from, say, the New Year's Eve chapter if you're planning a New Year's Eve party – mix and match recipes, craft projects and hairstyles to suit your tastes.

**3** Complement or expand your event-planning with recipes and tips from my first book, *The Vintage Tea Party Book* (shameless plug!).

Then, all there is left to do is to eat, drink, love, laugh and be armed and prepared in the kitchen, so that you can thoroughly enjoy your tea party and hold onto the memory of it forever.

A fantastic hen party we hosted, with the love of my life, Mr Strawbridge, 2010.

Hosting a fabulous Christmas party, 2011.

# MY JOURNEY

I like old things. Old-fashioned, one-of-a-kind, hand-picked items charm me with their uniqueness and personality in a way that only something with history can.

My journey started at 13 years of age, when I began thrifting in local car boot sales. People sold their old junk out of the back of their cars, and my heart would race whenever I found a jewel, which was often very cheap. I became more attached to some items than others, and learned that certain things could fetch a decent amount of money for an East London girl like me, so in my early 20s I became a hospitable vintage dealer. I established a regular event called the Angel-A Vintage Experience, where I sold my finds, but also fed and watered the public in order to create the ultimate shopping experience!

Hosting is in my blood. My warm, giving parents, whose pictures are shown here, are wonderful role models. When I was a child they were always feeding people in our family home, which eventually led to them owning an incredibly special restaurant full of love and great British food.

In 2007 the Angel-A Vintage Experience came to an end, and it seemed the most natural thing in the world to follow my parents' example and change the direction of my business towards hosting. The Vintage Patisserie was born.

I'm incredibly blessed to have hosted so many memorable events, from weddings, bar mitzvahs and birthday parties for all ages to hen parties, baby showers and even a very memorable tea for two in the back of my London cab! Each event is unique and I feel electrified by people's happiness. I hope this book gives you the tools you need to touch people in the same way for any event that life throws at you – there really is a vintage tea-party spread that can fit the bill, no matter what the occasion.

Above: Nan and Grandad,
serving in WWII, 1943.

Right: Great Grandfather
having a good time, 1951.

Below: My dad (centre) playing the Mad Hatter in his school play, 1959.

Right: My dad aged 13 at the bar my uncle made, 1963.

Above: Me as a baby, very happy to be holding an apple, 1978.

Above: Mum and Dad on their wedding day, 1969.

Below: My brother and me at Christmas, 1982.

Right: My mum, dad and brother at a family wedding, 1976.

# THE PRESENT

It has been quite a year for me and the Vintage Patisserie. After 12 years of working from a converted school house in East London (which doubled as my home), we have moved to a fabulously quirky space just down the road in Hackney, where we now host the majority of our events. On a personal level, I've spent the year being quite sickeningly in love! (You'll notice the odd mention of the man himself in these pages.) I've learned how to balance this love with the rest of my life as a friend, daughter and boss, and have watched my company grow and blossom.

When my first book, *The Vintage Tea Party Book*, was released last year, I felt incredibly nervous! My life's work was suddenly available to the public to critique, but I was blown away by the amazing response it received and I still pinch myself every day to make sure I'm not dreaming! My friends, family and publisher all felt incredibly proud when it was shortlisted in the food and drink category at the National Book Awards in 2011 – a truly magical night that I will never forget!

I've also spent the year crafting and styling this new book. Each recipe is lovingly tested and tasted, and each image has its own unique story and mood, and is brought to life with vintage props, kitchenalia and clothes. And I have met some truly wonderful people while working on the book, from Jon, the ex-clown who showed me around his circus and introduced to me to his wife, a former acrobat, to the excitable bunch of young ladies I took shopping for vintage-style outfits for the Coming of Age chapter. This book was put together with love and I hope this shows on every page.

Left: Gizzi Erskine and me at the launch of my first book, 2011.

Below: The Vintage Patisserie ladies hosting an Urban tea party at the flagship Puma store, 2012.

Above: Me, Zandra Rhodes and my right-hand lady Lauren, 2011. (I wore a vintage Zandra Rhodes dress on the cover of book 1, so it was a total honour to host a party for her!)

Left: Me at the Galaxy Book Awards, 2011.

# YOUR JOURNEY

Throwing a fabulous party is about creating a vision and bringing it to life. When you start to plan a party, you embark on your own unique journey, and when the guests begin to arrive, you take them along for the ride, too! This book is here for inspiration. But if you and I were sharing a pot of tea and a chat and you asked if I had any tips to ensure your party goes with a big bang, this is what I would say:

"**Always start your journey with an invite.** It will set the mood for the party and spark the excitement from the moment the envelope is opened! At the beginning of each chapter you will find a ready-made invitation. Feel free to photocopy it and use it as your own, or download it from *www.vintagepatisserie.co.uk*.

**Plan your menu with price, production and serving capability in mind.** Do you have the right pots, plates, and so on? If not, get down to your local charity shop! A spectacular tea party can be achieved on any budget.

**Do something personal for your guests.** It'll be the one memory that will stay with them always.

**Ensure you are fully prepared.** This means you'll be able to spend party time with your loved ones, rather than just in the kitchen!

**Finish with a thank you.** It ends the journey with style and warmth and makes a great final page in your photo album! Photocopy the ready-made thank you cards at the beginning of each chapter and use them as your own, or download them from *www.vintagepatisserie.co.uk*."

On that note, thank you for coming on this journey with me, and I raise my teacup to you:

"To your perfect tea-party year. May it bring health and happiness to you and all those you get drunk with – I mean, that you host!"

Love Angel ♥

NEW YEAR'S EVE TEA PARTY

The 31st of December is an incredibly important day in the calendar year. For me, it's often my only downtime, so I've made it totally mine, to spend with my loved ones and spoil them rotten. On New Year's Eve, I love to reflect on the year gone by and to set my goals and intentions for the year ahead. There is no better way of celebrating the past and the future than by living in the now and basking in a glittering evening of glamour and decadence. Start as you mean to go on? I wish!

# Happy New Year

# Good Luck in the New Year!

Pigeon is a wonderful meat: it has hardly any fat and is full of gamey flavour. Cooked with woody mushrooms in a sweet red wine sauce, this light pithivier is divine. Pithivier is just a fancy name for pie, by the way. It's New Year, after all – I can't serve pie! If your man won't go out and shoot pigeon, shop-bought duck is a great alternative. For non meat-eaters, the pithivier is a great cooking platform for anything, including desserts.

MAKES 6

PREP 25 mins, plus marinating

COOK 40 mins

# WILD MUSHROOM & PIGEON BREAST PITHIVIERS

6 pigeon breasts (approx. 250g/9oz total weight), shot removed

750g (1lb 10oz) shop-bought all-butter puff pastry

plain flour, for dusting

1 tbsp olive oil

200g (7oz) wild mushrooms, sliced

30g (1oz) butter

2 garlic cloves, finely chopped

1 free-range egg, beaten

**For the marinade**

1 garlic clove, crushed

leaves from 3 sprigs of thyme

6 black peppercorns, crushed

3 tbsp extra-virgin olive oil

**For the red wine sauce**

2 tbsp granulated sugar

200ml (1/3 pint) red wine

2 sprigs of thyme

6 juniper berries, lightly crushed

salt and black pepper

**1** For the marinade, combine the garlic, thyme leaves, peppercorns and olive oil in a small bowl. Using a sharp knife, score the skin of the pigeon breasts lightly and rub in the marinade. Marinate in the refrigerator for at least 20 minutes.

**2** Meanwhile, preheat the oven to 180°C/fan 160ºC/gas mark 4. Roll out the pastry on a floured surface to a thickness of 3mm (1/8in). Cut out 12 × 10cm- (4in-) rounds.

**3** Heat the olive oil in a frying pan set over a medium-high heat. Sauté the mushrooms for 5 minutes, then add the butter and garlic and cook for 2 minutes more. Transfer to a sieve set over a bowl to allow any juices to drain out. Put the pan back on the hob, increase the heat and sear the pigeon-breast skin for 1½ minutes each side to brown, then set aside for 5 minutes to rest.

**4** Place a few mushrooms in the centres of 6 of the pastry rounds. Trim the breasts so that they sit inside a circle that has a diameter of about 7cm (2¾in) – use a pastry cutter as a guide. Top with more of the mushrooms, brush around the edges with the beaten egg and cover with the remaining pastry rounds. Seal by lightly crimping the edges and decorate with spiral lines drawn with the point of a knife from the centre outwards.

**5** Glaze the pastry with the egg wash and bake for 25 minutes or until golden brown.

**6** Meanwhile, to make the red wine sauce, combine the sugar and a few drops of water in a small, clean saucepan set over a high heat. Once the sugar melts and has become a dark golden brown, pour in the red wine. Add the thyme and the juniper berries. Cook the sauce for about 12–15 minutes until it is reduced by two-thirds. Season to taste, strain and serve warm alongside the pithiviers.

I once heard that the chartreuse took its name from the Carthusian order of monks, who were vegetarians. The story states that the monks would hide forbidden meat in the centre of the dish, enabling them to indulge. Naughty! It's a stunning dish that is incredibly satisfying to make. I will only make this on special occasions, and love doing so on New Year's Eve while reflecting on my year and getting excited about what's ahead.

# MINI CHARTREUSE OF VEGETABLES

**MAKES** 6

**PREP** 30 mins, plus chilling

**COOK** 17–22 mins

60ml (2¼fl oz) double cream

300g (10½oz) potatoes, peeled, boiled and well drained

salt and pepper

½ butternut squash, peeled, boiled and well drained

3 large carrots, cut into sticks

300g (10½oz) fine beans or asparagus tips, trimmed

150g (5½oz) Brussels sprouts, bases trimmed and leaves separated

75g (2¾oz) garden peas

butter, for greasing

100g (3½oz) mature Cheddar cheese, grated

**1** Add half the cream to the cooked and drained potatoes and mash them until smooth, seasoning to taste. Do the same for the butternut squash. The 2 mashes should feel quite stiff.

**2** Trim the carrot sticks and beans or asparagus to fit the height of a 125ml-(4fl oz-)capacity ramekin. Parboil all the vegetables separately for about 2 minutes. Drain and rinse under cold water, then leave to dry.

**3** Place a round of nonstick baking paper in the bottom of each of 6 ramekins and butter the sides thickly – don't skimp with the butter at this stage! Arrange the carrots and beans or asparagus alternately around the edge. Add enough peas to cover the base of each dish. Now layer up the potatoes, Brussels sprouts, cheese and squash until you reach the top of the ramekin. Place the ramekins in the refrigerator for about 20 minutes to allow the butter to become firm. Preheat the oven to 180°C/fan 160°C/gas mark 4.

**4** Place the ramekins on a baking tray and bake for 15–20 minutes, then remove them from the oven and allow to set for 3–5 minutes before inverting onto serving dishes. If necessary, loosen the sides of the chartreuse from the ramekins with a sharp knife before turning out.

Your guests may not want to eat this dish for fear of spoiling its elegant beauty. But an exciting journey begins the moment their taste buds experience the luxurious textures and flavour of the ballettes, and they will taste all the love and hard work you put into getting them to the table. Be warned – these are such a force for indulgence, your guests may end up jumping fully clothed into a bath full of Champagne, screaming "Happy New Year!"

# Fois Gras Ballettes

MAKES 6

PREP 1 hour, plus cooling and chilling

COOK 11–15 mins

250ml (9fl oz) chicken consommé

1 × 12g (½oz) sachet gelatine

100g (3½oz) foie gras (or faux gras – *see* note, below)

100g (3½oz) watercress, to serve

**For the egg garnish**

4 free-range eggs, separated

2½ tbsp double cream

salt

butter, for greasing

red food colouring

**1** In a small saucepan, pour the chicken consommé over the gelatine and leave it to sit for 5 minutes. Set the pan over a low heat until the gelatine dissolves; do not let it boil. Take the pan off the heat and set aside to allow the contents to cool to room temperature.

**2** To make the white egg garnish, mix the egg whites with 1 tablespoon of the cream and a pinch of salt. Beat the mixture well, then pour into greased dariole moulds (we used 3 moulds with 6cm/2½in bases). You want only a thin layer in each mould. Put roughly 5cm (2in) boiling water in a pan, add the moulds, ensuring no water can enter them, and poach for 3–5 minutes until firm. Turn it out to cool and, when cold, cut or stamp out the mixture in fancy shapes (we used star-shaped cutters).

**3** To make the pink egg garnish, mix 3 egg yolks with the remaining 1½ tablespoons cream and a pinch of salt. Add a few drops of food colouring to make the mixture turn light pink and beat well. Mould and poach the mixture as you did with the white egg garnish. Turn it out to cool, then cut or stamp out fancy shapes.

**4** Pour some of the gelatine mixture (aspic jelly) into 6 half-sphere moulds, each with a diameter of 6cm (2½in), and swirl it around to cover the interior. This will hold the garnish in place. Using the shaped egg garnish, decorate around the sides of the moulds. Leave to set in the refrigerator for 20 minutes.

**5** Place a tablespoon of fois gras in the centre of each mould to add another layer. Arrange some egg garnish over this, top with another layer of liquid aspic jelly to fill the mould, then chill for 20 minutes until firm.

**6** Dip each mould into hot water and turn out the ballettes onto a bed of watercress to serve.

**Note** To avoid using foie gras, make "faux gras". Mellow some duck or chicken livers by soaking them overnight in milk with some garlic, thyme, salt and pepper. Dry the livers, sear them in a hot pan for 2 minutes (the centres should still be pink), then process with half their weight of soft butter until smooth. Adjust the seasoning and chill until set. The resulting faux gras is silky smooth.

**SERVES** 6

**PREP** 20 mins

**COOK** 45 mins

A few dishes that I passionately adore live in my "only-for-highly-momentous-occasions" category. One such occasion is Mother's Day, a special business achievement would be another, and New Year's Eve is the last. Rationing this particular delicacy allows me to appreciate the flavour of the sea all over again each time I get to taste it. Lobster Bisque is a classic French dish that celebrates the lobster by cooking it in its shell to extract and deepen every last morsel of flavour. It's a dish that will impress and, as long as you don't overcook the lobster, you can't go wrong!

# Lobster Bisque

1 medium lobster

30g (1oz) butter

1 onion, finely chopped

4 garlic cloves, crushed

125ml (4fl oz) white wine

4 tsp Worcestershire sauce

2 tsp Tabasco sauce

½ tsp dried thyme

60ml (2¼fl oz) brandy

500ml (18fl oz) hot water

500ml (18fl oz) whole milk

2 tsp smoked sweet paprika

4 tbsp tomato purée

4 bay leaves

50g (1¾oz) white long-grain rice

500ml (18fl oz) double cream, plus extra to serve (optional)

salt and black pepper

**1** Remove the flesh from the lobster shell (or ask your fishmonger to do this for you), chop the lobster shell into large pieces and set the meat aside. In a large saucepan, heat the butter over a low heat and cook the lobster shells and the onion for about 7 minutes until soft and translucent. Add the garlic and cook for about 2 minutes more.

**2** Increase the heat to high and add the white wine to the pan. Cook the wine for about 1 minute, meanwhile dislodging all the tasty residue in the pan so that it combines with the mixture.

**3** Add the Worcestershire and Tabasco sauces and the thyme and sauté for another minute, then add the brandy and stir.

**4** Add the hot water, milk, paprika, tomato purée and bay leaves and stir well.

**5** Next, add the rice and allow the mixture to come to a gentle boil. Simmer for about 25 minutes until the rice is cooked.

**6** Remove the lobster shells and bay leaves and discard them. Purée the soup using a hand-held blender, or by passing it through a sieve, pushing the mixture through the mesh to purée it.

**7** When the mixture is smooth and velvety, return it to the pan and set it over a low heat. Add the lobster meat and cook gently until the soup is heated through. Then whisk in the cream, if using, and simmer just until the soup is warmed through; don't let it come to the boil.

**8** Add salt and pepper to taste. If desired, add a blob of cream in the middle of the soup bowl and swirl to serve.

# HOW TO COOK YOUR LOBSTER

**WHAT IF YOUR LOBSTER IS STILL SWIMMING?**
The firm white meat of lobster is sweet and succulent. It's available all year round and it is widely agreed that lobster from colder waters has the best flavour. There are 3 main types. The best flavoured is the European lobster, from around Britain, Ireland, Northern France and Scandinavia. Then there is the Canadian or American; these have round, very fleshy claws. Finally, the Slipper or Squat lobsters live in warmer oceans, such as those surrounding Australia.

Before they are cooked, lobsters are very dark in colour and range from blue/green to red/purple. However, when they are cooked, they turn a distinctive bright red colour.

**CHOOSING YOUR LOBSTER**
The lobster that's easiest to use is shop-bought, freshly cooked, split in half and already cleaned. If you have a choice, go for the one with the brightest-coloured shell, and that has the tail curled under the body (when cooked alive, the tails curl under).

For the freshest meat, buy a whole live lobster. Obviously, you need to choose the liveliest you can find, and its tail should definitely curl back under if you straighten it out. A frisky lobster is a fresh lobster.

A little care is necessary when handling lobsters: the plates on the tail move across each other when the tail opens and closes and the claws are seriously sharp and should be secured with elastic bands.

**EXTRACTING THE FLESH**
If you buy the lobster halved and freshly cooked, it's ready to eat. You may need to crack open the claws using a hammer, a pair of lobster crackers or the back of a heavy cook's knife to get at the meat.

Live lobsters should be killed before cooking. The most humane way to kill your lobster is to put it into the freezer for a couple of hours, rendering it unconscious. Wrap it in a tea towel so that it can't move, then push the tip of a large, sharp knife through the centre of its head (there is a cross shape on the head that marks the spot) about 2–3cm (¾–1¼in) behind the eyes.

Put the lobster into a large saucepan of salted cold water and slowly bring it to the boil. When the water has reached boiling point, reduce the heat and simmer the lobster for around 15 minutes for the first 450g (1lb). Simmer for a further 10 minutes for each extra 450g (1lb), for up to a maximum of 40 minutes. When the lobster is cooked, its shell will turn a deep brick red. Drain off the water and leave the lobster to cool.

To get the flesh out, first twist off the claws, then break into sections, crack the claw shell and remove the flesh. Twist off the legs from the body, flatten with the back of a knife and then use a pick or a teaspoon handle to remove the flesh.

Now sort out the body. To split the lobster in half along its length, insert a large, sharp knife and press down firmly. The body and tail should split lengthways. Then cut through the head in the same way. You should now be able to separate the 2 halves. Remove and discard the pale stomach sac, the gills and the dark intestinal thread along the length of the tail. The green pasty stuff in the body (or the "tomalley"), which is both its liver and pancreas, is considered a delicacy. Remove the tail meat and scrape out the soft flesh from the shell.

There may be coral-coloured roe present. Mix this with butter to make lobster butter, which is lovely on toast or added to sauces. Use leftover shells for stock.

These choux-pastry beauties are my secret weapons for showing off! The butterscotch is also a real treat. Did you know that swans are sometimes monogamous for their whole lives? I am so romanced by this idea! It really gets me in the mood for that magical midnight moment when I must kiss the first person I see... Pucker up!

# CHOUX PASTRY SWANS

MAKES 6

PREP 45 mins, plus cooling

COOK 25 mins

50g (1¾oz) butter, plus extra for greasing

60g (2¼oz) strong white flour

1 tsp caster sugar

2 free-range eggs, beaten

150ml (¼ pint) double cream

**For the butterscotch sauce**

50g (1¾oz) butter

50g (1¾oz) dark brown soft sugar

50g (1¾oz) golden syrup

1 tbsp lemon juice

75ml (2½fl oz) double cream

edible gold lustre spray (available online, optional)

**1** Preheat the oven to 180°C/fan 160°C/gas mark 4.

**2** To make the choux pastry, melt the butter in 150ml (¼ pint) water in a small saucepan over a medium heat and bring to a full boil. Immediately add all the flour and sugar in one go and stir continuously with a wooden spoon for a couple of minutes until the mixture pulls away from the side of the pan, forming a ball. Take the pan off the heat and continue stirring for 1 minute while the mixture cools.

**3** Add the eggs, one by one, mixing the dough well to ensure each egg is thoroughly incorporated before adding the next. The mixture should be smooth and glossy.

**4** To make the swan bodies, spoon the pastry mixture into a piping bag fitted with a plain medium-sized nozzle. Pipe 6 mounds, each the equivalent of a tablespoon of the mixture, onto a greased baking sheet, set about 8cm (3¼in) apart.

**5** Flatten each mound slightly with a fork dipped in water. Bake for about 15 minutes until the choux puffs are golden brown and sound hollow when tapped. Cool on a wire rack.

**6** To make the swan heads and necks, fit a piping bag with a small plain nozzle and pipe S-shapes, each about 5cm (2in) long, onto a lightly greased baking sheet. Pinch the beginning of each "S" to make a beak. Bake for about 8 minutes until the choux puffs are golden brown. Take care not to burn them. Cool on a wire rack.

**7** In an electric mixer, whip the cream until firm peaks form. Set aside in the refrigerator.

**8** For the wings, slice the top off each body with a serrated knife. Cut the tops in half lengthways. Set aside.

**9** Pipe the cream into the cavity of each choux puff, finishing about 5cm (2in) above the top of the pastry.

**10** Insert 2 wings, rounded edges down, into the centre of each filling so that they form a V-shape. Insert the S-shaped neck into the cream.

**11** To make the sauce, put the butter, sugar and syrup into a saucepan and bring to a gentle simmer. Take the pan off the heat, add the lemon juice and stir. Stir in the cream. To give the sauce a glittery shimmer, spray it with gold lustre when in situ on a serving platter.

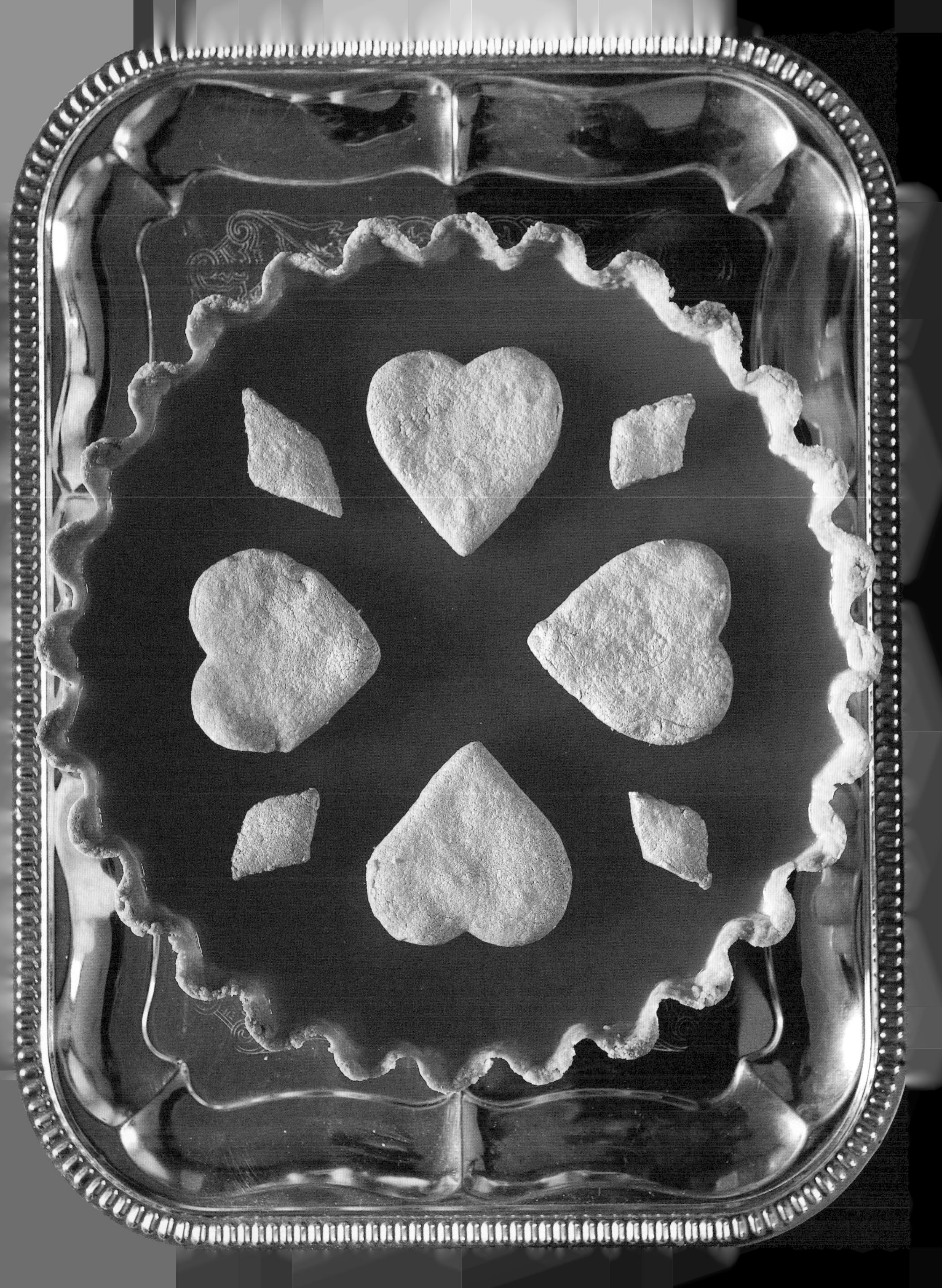

Do you remember the part in *Alice in Wonderland* where Alice meets the Queen of Hearts? There is an explosion of dancing cards, just before the sentence of "Off with her head". Well, this tart reminds me of that crazy scene. It is perfect for celebrating a special occasion and will make your guests want to dive in. And while it looks highly indulgent, it is actually incredibly refreshing to the palate after lots of rich savoury food.

# Queen of Heart's Tart

**For the pastry**

500g (1lb 2oz) plain flour, plus extra for dusting

100g (3½oz) icing sugar

250g (9oz) butter, chilled and cubed

2 free-range eggs, beaten

splash of milk (optional)

edible gold lustre spray (available online, optional)

**For the raspberry jelly**

2 leaves gelatine

500g (1lb 2oz) frozen raspberries

30g (1oz) caster sugar

**SERVES 12**

**PREP 30** mins, plus chilling

**COOK 25** mins

1 Sift the flour and icing sugar into a bowl. Rub in the butter. When the mixture resembles breadcrumbs, mix in the eggs, adding some milk if the mixture still looks dry. Bring the dough together into a ball with your hands. Wrap it in clingfilm and chill for 30 minutes.

2 Preheat the oven to 170°C/fan 150°C/gas mark 3½. Roll out the dough on a lightly floured surface and use it to line a 23cm (9in) loose-bottomed fluted tart tin. Use pastry cutters to cut out heart and diamond shapes from the remaining pastry to decorate the tart. Put these on a baking sheet. Cover the lined tart tin with nonstick baking paper and fill it with baking beans. Bake for 15 minutes, then remove the biscuits from the oven and the paper and beans from the tart case and bake the case for a further 5 minutes. Allow it to cool. Spray the biscuits with gold lustre, if using, once cool.

3 To make the jelly, cover the gelatine with a little cold water and soak it until softened. Put the raspberries, sugar and 1 litre (1¾ pints) water in a saucepan. Heat the mixture gently until the sugar has dissolved, then simmer for a couple of minutes. Push it through a sieve into a clean pan, heat a little, then add the gelatine leaves (squeezing out the excess water) and leave until dissolved. Strain into a jug and leave to cool.

4 Pour the jelly into the pastry, refrigerate for 3 hours and top with biscuits to serve.

At all momentous occasions I would expect every guest to have something to take home with them to eat the next day. (No one would dream of not having a wedding cake, right?) So this is my New Year's version. Using festive flavours that are light after an indulgent evening, this bundt is not only show-stopping to look at, but delicious, too.

# CLEMENTINE & COINTREAU SYRUP BUNDT CAKE

**SERVES 16**

**PREP 20** mins, plus cooling

**COOK 1** hour–**1** hour **20** mins

360g (12½oz) unsalted butter, softened, plus extra for greasing

450g (1lb) caster sugar

6 large free-range eggs, lightly beaten

grated rind of 6 clementines

500g (1lb 2oz) self-raising flour, plus extra for dusting

8 tbsp clementine juice

edible gold lustre spray (available online, optional)

**For the syrup**

thin strips of rind (no pith) from 1 clementine

8 tbsp clementine juice

200g (7oz) icing sugar

75ml (2½fl oz) orange liqueur

1 Preheat oven to 180°C/fan 160°C/gas mark 4. Grease a large cathedral bundt cake mould (we used one that was 21cm/8¼in in diameter and 10cm/4in deep), lightly dust it with flour and set it aside.

2 Cream the butter and sugar together with a wooden spoon or an electric whisk until light and fluffy, then slowly add the eggs and grated clementine rind, beating well after each addition. Fold in the flour, then the clementine juice, and spoon the mixture into the prepared bundt tin.

3 Bake for 1 hour–1 hour 20 minutes until a skewer inserted into the middle comes out with just a few moist crumbs stuck to it. You may need to cover it after about 45 minutes of cooking to stop it becoming too brown. Set it on a wire rack to cool for 15 minutes, then turn out the cake and prick it all over with a cocktail stick or skewer.

4 While the cake is cooling, make the syrup. Place the strips of clementine rind and juice in a saucepan with the icing sugar and heat gently until the sugar has completely dissolved.

5 Boil the syrup for another 2–3 minutes, then remove from the heat and strain out the rind. Finally, add the orange liqueur. Spoon the syrup evenly over the cake. Leave the bundt to sit until the syrup has been absorbed, then spray it with edible gold lustre, if using, to give it a shimmery finish.

Black Bun is a traditional Scottish treat, originally reserved for Twelfth Night, but now served during the New Year festivities. It is a rich, moist fruitcake baked in a pastry crust. When it's made well, the fruit will stick to the knife when cut. Ensure you make this a few weeks before New Year's Eve so that the fruits absorb the alcohol and the cake matures to full flavour.

# Traditional Black Bun

**SERVES 10**

**PREP 25** mins, plus chilling and maturing

**COOK 2** hours

1 free-range egg, lightly beaten

about 2 tbsp milk

**For the pastry**

200g (7oz) plain flour, plus extra for dusting

½ tsp baking powder

pinch of salt

50g (1¾oz) butter, chilled and cubed

50g (1¾oz) white vegetable fat or lard, chilled and cubed

**For the filling**

200g (7oz) plain flour

200g (7oz) raisins

200g (7oz) currants

100g (3½oz) flaked almonds

100g (3½oz) chopped mixed peel

75g (2¾oz) dark muscovado sugar

2 tbsp black treacle

2 tbsp brandy or whisky, plus extra for brushing

1 tsp ground mixed spice

1 tsp ground cinnamon

1 tsp ground ginger

½ tsp black pepper

½ tsp bicarbonate of soda

**1** To make the pastry, put the flour, baking powder and salt in a bowl. Add the butter and fat and rub with your fingertips until the mixture resembles breadcrumbs. Stir in 4 tablespoons cold water and mix to a soft dough. Wrap in clingfilm and chill it in the refrigerator while you make the filling.

**2** Preheat the oven to 160°C/fan 140°C/gas mark 3. Mix the filling ingredients together with most of the beaten egg in a large bowl, adding enough milk to just moisten the mixture.

**3** Dust a clean work surface with flour. Roll out three-quarters of the dough to a rectangle large enough to line the base and sides of a 900g (2lb) loaf tin, approximately 23cm × 13cm (9in × 5in). Drape the dough into the tin and press it up against the sides, smoothing out any creases. Tightly pack in the filling and press it down well. Brush the top of the fruit mixture with some brandy or whisky.

**4** Roll out the remaining dough to a rectangle large enough to fit the top of the lined tin. Dampen the edges of the pastry in the tin with water, press the pastry lid on top and seal them well. Crimp the edges, if desired.

**5** With a skewer, make 4 holes through the top of the pastry right down to the bottom of the tin, then use a fork to prick the surface all over. Brush the lid with the remaining beaten egg.

**6** Bake for 2 hours. To prevent the bun browning too quickly, cover with aluminium foil or nonstick baking paper towards the end of the cooking time. Allow it to cool on a wire rack in the tin for 1 hour.

**7** When cold, carefully turn out the bun onto foil. Use more foil to wrap it, then store it in an airtight container. Keep for at least 10 days in a cool, dry place before cutting the cake or it will fall apart.

New Year's Eve is the occasion for the biggest toast of the year. The entire world is celebrating together – how special is that? These are my favourite New Year tipples. They use traditional drinks you would expect to be served on such a momentous night, but also celebrate and mix in festive and seasonal ingredients. "Please raise your glass – may all your troubles during the coming year last only for as long as your New Year's resolutions!"

# MULLED WHITE WINE SANGRIA

SERVES 6

PREP 25 mins, plus optional chilling

COOK 20–25 mins

110ml (3¾fl oz) honey, preferably orange-blossom

rind of 2 lemons, cut into long strips

60ml (2¼fl oz) freshly squeezed lemon juice

4 star anise

4 cinnamon sticks

12 cloves

2 bottles of dry white wine, such as Sauvignon Blanc

225ml (8fl oz) orange Muscat

1 apple, cored, halved and thinly sliced

1 pear, cored, halved and thinly sliced

2 lemons, thinly sliced crossways

12 kumquats, thinly sliced crossways

ice cubes (optional)

**1** Bring 225ml (8fl oz) water, the honey, lemon rind and juice, star anise, cinnamon sticks and cloves to a simmer in a large saucepan set over a medium heat. Reduce the heat to low and cook for 15 minutes.

**2** To serve cold, mix the spice mixture, wines and fruit in a large pitcher. Cover and refrigerate overnight. Transfer the mixture to a large punch bowl and serve the drink with ice. To serve hot, heat the spice mixture and wines in a large saucepan over a low heat until heated through. Add the fruit and divide up between 6 mugs.

# Lemon Drop Champagne Punch

3 lemons

125g (4½oz) caster sugar

1 × 750ml bottle of Champagne, chilled

175ml (6fl oz) best-quality vodka, chilled

**SERVES** 6

**PREP** 20 mins, plus cooling

**COOK** 5 mins

**1** Using a vegetable peeler, remove the rind from each lemon, working around the fruit in a long, continuous spiral. Juice the lemons and strain the pulp (you should have 175ml/6fl oz juice). Set aside.

**2** Heat the sugar with 125ml (4fl oz) water in a small saucepan set over a low heat, stirring until the sugar has dissolved. Bring the mixture to the boil, then take the pan off the heat. Add the lemon rind, then set the syrup aside for about 2 hours to cool completely.

**3** Pour the Champagne, vodka, lemon juice and syrup into a jug. Stir and pour the drink into a decanter or punch bowl.

# Countdown Cocktail

50ml (2fl oz) gin

75ml (2½fl oz) blood orange juice

ice cubes

2 dashes of Angostura bitters

slice of blood orange, to garnish

**SERVES** 1

**PREP** 5 mins

**1** Pour the gin and orange juice into an old-fashioned glass filled with ice cubes. Stir well.

**2** Add the Angostura bitters and stir again. Decorate the drink with a slice of blood orange, then serve.

Lemon Drop Champagne Punch

Countdown Cocktail

Mulled White Wine Sangria

# HOW TO CREATE
# THE VICTORIANA

Make it your New Year's resolution to experiment and find the perfect vintage-look hairstyle for you. Here, I've taken inspiration from the Victorian era; think curled, coiffured hair and romantic up-dos. Believe it or not, this style is really easy to achieve. The most important thing is to first curl the hair tightly with as many curls as possible. If you need more volume, try adding a hair rat or rat roll, which you can buy in pharmacies and online – or try making your own!

## YOU WILL NEED

❧ hairspray ❧ curling tongs ❧ section clips ❧ tail comb ❧ Kirby grips
❧ hair rat ❧ hairpins ❧ flowers and decorative hair slides

△ **STEP 1** Spray the hair with hairspray, then use the curling tongs to curl your hair into small, tight sections. Use the section clips to hold each curl while it cools. For this look I used 3 curls around the hairline away from the face, 22 curls at the back and 4 larger curls on top to create a soft wave.

△ **STEP 2** Once the curls have cooled, remove the clips but do not brush out the curls. Part the hair roughly through the centre and, using Kirby grips, secure the hair rat by pinning it at the base where it meets the head, and at the crown of the head.

△ **STEP 3** Backcomb the hair around the rat using a tail comb. Sweep it up in variously sized sections to disguise the rat and pin it in place. Once the rat is covered, pin the rest of the curls in place. Don't be too neat; this is a romantic look. Sweep the front away from your face and hide the ends in the curls around the rat.

◁ **STEP 4** To finish, add flowers, decorative hair slides – in fact, add whatever you want. This look should be completely over the top and playful!

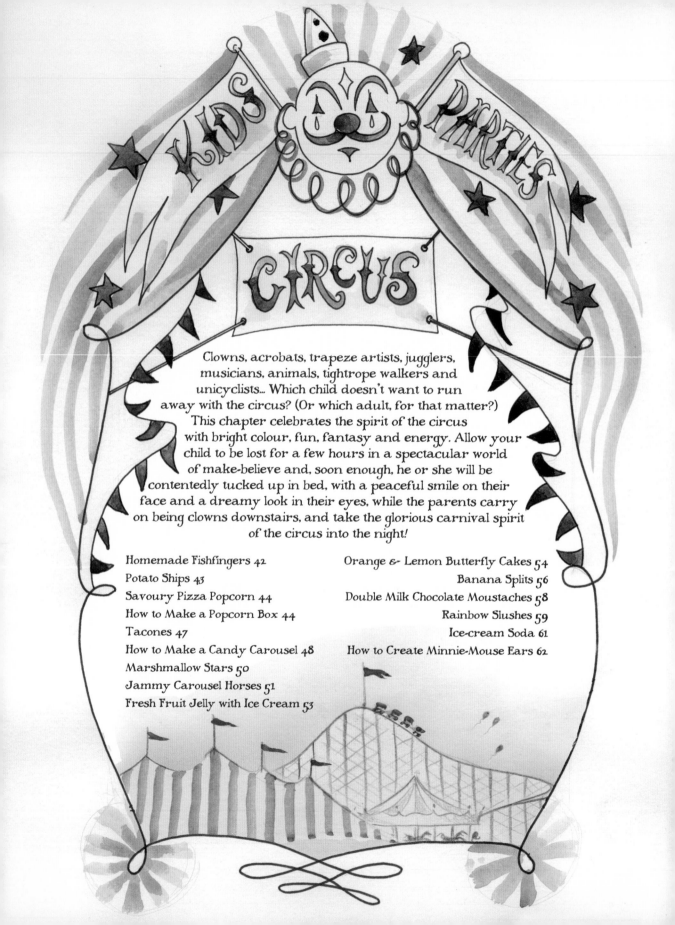

# KIDS PARTIES

# CIRCUS

Clowns, acrobats, trapeze artists, jugglers, musicians, animals, tightrope walkers and unicyclists... Which child doesn't want to run away with the circus? (Or which adult, for that matter?) This chapter celebrates the spirit of the circus with bright colour, fun, fantasy and energy. Allow your child to be lost for a few hours in a spectacular world of make-believe and, soon enough, he or she will be contentedly tucked up in bed, with a peaceful smile on their face and a dreamy look in their eyes, while the parents carry on being clowns downstairs, and take the glorious carnival spirit of the circus into the night!

Fishfingers and chips was the meal of choice when my mum was pushed for time. I won't blame her for cooking shop-bought but, cooked fresh, the crunch of breadcrumbs with the flaky fish will be loved by all. Check out our cute custom-made cartons (*see page 44*), ideal for fishfingers and chips.

# HOMEMADE FISHFINGERS

SERVES **6**

PREP **10** mins

COOK **20** mins

400g (14oz) skinless sustainable white fish

1 free-range egg

85g (3oz) white breadcrumbs, made from day-old bread

rind and juice of 1 lemon

½ tsp dried oregano

salt and black pepper

3 tbsp olive oil

tomato ketchup, to serve

**1** Preheat the oven to 180°C/fan 160°C/gas mark 4. Slice the fish into strips that are about 2cm (¾in) wide and 8cm (3¼in) long. Beat the egg in a small bowl. Tip the breadcrumbs onto a plate and mix in the lemon rind along with the oregano and some salt and pepper.

**2** Gently heat the oil in a nonstick frying pan. Working in batches, dip the fish strips into the egg, then roll them in the seasoned breadcrumbs and fry for a minute or so on each side until golden. Transfer the fish to a baking sheet and bake for 10 minutes until cooked through. Serve immediately with tomato ketchup.

I believe the love of potatoes begins at birth, but I would feel guilty serving up a spud without the fun factor! When I saw these ships at a grown man's nautical-themed party, I just had to borrow the idea. Sail on with any topping of your choice.

SERVES **12**

PREP **15** mins

COOK **25–30** mins

# POTATO SHIPS

12 mini potatoes (Charlotte work well)

4 thin slices of ham

2 cherry tomatoes

60g (2¼oz) Cheddar cheese, grated

**1** Preheat the oven to 200°C/fan 180°C/gas mark 6. Bake the potatoes on a baking sheet for 25–30 minutes. Meanwhile, cut the ham into little triangles. Quarter the cherry tomatoes, then halve widthways. Skewer the ham and tomato pieces onto cocktail sticks, as shown in the picture, to make the sails.

**2** Remove the potatoes from the oven and, when cool enough to handle, slice off the tops. Scatter over the cheese and place the sails on top. Serve immediately.

For a healthy yet tasty belly-filler, popcorn is the perfect snack. Add some delicious pizza-inspired spices, make a simple popcorn box with our circus-themed design (*see* below) and let the fun begin! Don't forget to individually label each bucket – kids will love to take these home with them to use again on cinema night.

# SAVOURY PIZZA POPCORN

SERVES **6**

PREP **10** mins

COOK **5** mins

2 tbsp vegetable oil

200g (7oz) popcorn kernels

2 tbsp grated Parmesan cheese

1 tsp garlic powder

1 tsp dried Italian herb seasoning

½ tsp sweet paprika

½ tsp salt

**1** Heat the oil in a large saucepan with a tight-fitting lid over a medium heat. Add the popcorn kernels, shake them around to coat them in the oil, then place the lid on the pan and leave it on the hob, shaking it occasionally, until there is about a 2- or 3-second gap between each pop.

**2** Meanwhile, combine the remaining ingredients in a large bowl. Remove the popcorn from the heat and toss it through the spices. Serve immediately, presented in personalized popcorn boxes.

# HOW TO MAKE A POPCORN BOX

**1** Photocopy the box template to the right, enlarging to your desired size. Cut out the photocopy and stick it onto card. Colour in the design, then cut out the shape.

**2** Score and fold along the lines as necessary, then fold the box into shape.

**3** Glue the flaps on the inside of the box. Allow to dry.

**4** Add some popcorn!

For added fun with a twist on the ice cream, these tacones are too cute for words, what with the tasty chicken, the crunch of the cone and the fresh salad. Feel free to change the filling to suit your own tastes.

SERVES **12**

PREP **20** mins, plus marinating

COOK **10** mins

# Tacones

2 tomatoes, coarsely chopped

juice of 1 lime

½ tsp salt

450g (1lb) boneless, skinless chicken thighs

3 corn tortillas

1 tbsp vegetable oil

½ tsp sweet paprika

½ tsp dried parsley

50g (1¾oz) Cheddar cheese, grated

**For the salsa**

½ avocado

½ onion

1 tomato

1 tbsp chopped fresh coriander leaves

**1** In a blender, purée the 2 tomatoes with the lime juice, 100ml (3½fl oz) water and the salt. Transfer the purée to a large bowl and add the chicken thighs. Cover with clingfilm and refrigerate for 6 hours or overnight.

**2** Preheat the oven to 200°C/fan 180°C/gas mark 6. Cut the tortillas into quarters and roll up each one to form a cone. Secure these with cocktail sticks, then place them on a baking sheet. Bake the cones for 5 minutes, then reshape them slightly, if necessary, before they cool. Place them on a wire rack, allow them to cool, then remove the cocktail sticks.

**3** Set the grill to high. Remove the chicken thighs from the marinade, pat them dry and place them on a grill pan. Brush with the oil and sprinkle with the paprika and parsley. Grill them for 10 minutes on each side until the chicken is lightly charred and cooked through.

**4** Meanwhile, make the salsa. Dice the avocado, onion and tomato, then toss them all together with the chopped coriander leaves.

**5** Transfer the chicken to your work surface and allow it to stand for 5 minutes. Cut the thighs into strips. Layer the chicken, cheese and salsa upright in the cones to assemble the tacones.

# How to make a
# candy carousel

I still remember my first time on a carousel and I've seen the cine footage that my mum took of me sitting on my dad's lap with the biggest smile on my face many times. You can make this carousel to delight the children, and hang delicious treats for them from it, such as the Marshmallow Stars and Jammy Carousel Horses on pages 50 and 51, to pull off.

## YOU WILL NEED

✖ 1 side plate (for a template) ✖ 1 saucer with a diameter at least 1cm (½in) smaller than your side plate (for a template) ✖ pen or pencil ✖ A2 sheet of white mount board, 2mm (1/16in) thick ✖ paper scissors ✖ string ✖ ruler ✖ cardboard tube from clingfilm/aluminium foil – its length should be equal to the height of your pencils + 6cm (2½in) ✖ glue gun ✖ coloured paints (optional) ✖ 6–7 sheets A4 paper in bright colours ✖ craft knife ✖ cutting mat ✖ bamboo skewers ✖ 1m (3ft) coloured ribbon, 3–4cm (1¼–1½in) wide (optional) ✖ treats for threading ✖ 5 unused pencils of one length ✖ glue stick ✖ hack saw ✖ sticky-backed paper (optional)

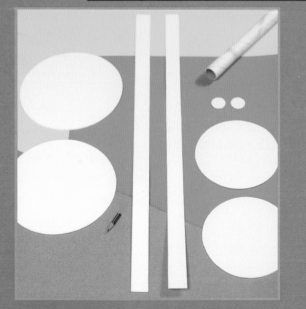

### CUT OUT THE MOUNT BOARD PIECES

**1** Using your side plate and saucer as templates, draw and then cut out 2 larger circles and 2 smaller circles from the mount board. Draw the circles close together, as you will need more mount board in step 4.

**2** Run the string around the circumference of 1 of your larger circles, then measure the piece of string to find the length of the circle's circumference.

**3** Mark out 2 strips on the mount board – each should be 3cm (1¼in) wide, and the length should be the same as the circumference of the larger circle. Cut out the strips.

**4** Draw around the end of your cardboard tube twice on the mount board to make 2 small circles. Cut out these circles and use the glue gun to attach 1 to each end of your tube.

## MAKE THE CAROUSEL CIRCLES

**1** Glue the long edge of 1 of the strips around the base of 1 of the larger circles, gluing and holding as you go. Repeat with the other strip and large circle.

**2** Using the end of your tube as a template, cut a circle bang in the centre of both smaller circles and 1 larger circle.

**3** Start decorating, as it is easier to do so before assembly. Paint the smaller circles or cover them with coloured paper.

**4** Take 1 small circle and, using the craft knife and cutting mat, make 4–6 small evenly spaced incisions 1cm (½in) from the outer rim. Attach bamboo skewers for the treats. It's easier to thread sweets onto them first, then position them on the carousel. Pass each skewer through an incision and secure with glue where it passes through. Or cut 4–6 lengths of ribbon that are long enough to be looped, yet will hang from the top of the carousel at a good height for treats to be strung onto them. Pass the aligned ends of each loop through 1 incision and knot them to secure it in place.

## MAKE THE CAROUSEL POLES

**1** Cut long 4cm- (1½in-) wide strips of coloured paper and apply glue to them. Roll up a pencil in a strip of paper, slowly pushing out air bubbles as you go. Repeat with 3 of the remaining 4 pencils. They will look slightly rectangular.

**2** Cut a long 3cm- (1¼in-) wide strip from 2 colours of A4 paper. Apply glue to 1 side of the first strip, then wrap it around the cardboard tube, working from the top down in a maypole effect. Apply glue to the second coloured strip and wrap the tube with this in the same way, covering any gaps.

**3** Carefully cut off the writing-end tip of the remaining pencil with a hack saw, about 2–3cm (¾–1¼in) from the sharpened tip. This tip will become the pivot on which the carousel spins. Using the glue gun, attach the pivot to 1 end of your tube, with the sharpened tip facing downwards.

## ASSEMBLE THE CAROUSEL

**1** The large circle without the hole will be the base of the carousel. Using your glue gun, attach the 4 covered pencils around the inside of the rim, spacing them evenly.

**2** Hold the inner tube in place so that the pencil tip rests in the middle of the base. Push the 2 smaller circles onto the

inner tube, starting with the one without the ribbons. (These will hang from the upper small circle.) The circles should fit snugly around the tube without sliding down along it, as the holes are just big enough for the tube to fit through.

**3** Push the remaining large circle onto the tube, leaving a few centimetres protruding at the top for a handle. Reach inside the top rim and glue the ends of the pencils to the inside of it. The main body is now complete – it should be a solid structure and the central pole should spin on the pencil pivot when turned by the handle.

**4** Now to make it look pretty! Be creative – we used paper and sticky-backed paper to add colour and pattern to our carousel. Use ribbon or paper and the glue gun to cover the handle and to add detail to the top of the carousel.

# MARSHMALLOW STARS

MAKES **24**

PREP **25** mins,
plus setting

COOK **15** mins

vegetable oil, for greasing
mixture of icing sugar and cornflour
(use equal proportions), for dusting
1 × 12g (½oz) sachet powdered gelatine
225g (8oz) caster sugar
1 tbsp liquid glucose
1 large free-range egg white
½ tsp vanilla extract

**1** Lightly grease 24 silicone star-shaped moulds (the ones we used were 4cm/1½in deep and 4cm/1½in wide) and dust with the icing sugar-and-cornflour mixture.

**2** Place the gelatine in a bowl. Boil a kettle, let it stand for 30 seconds, then pour 75ml (2½fl oz) water over the gelatine and stir until it has dissolved.

**3** Put the caster sugar, glucose and 200ml (⅓ pint) water into a heavy-based saucepan. Warm over a low heat until the sugar dissolves, then increase the heat and boil until the temperature of the sugar syrup reaches 125°C (257°F) on a sugar thermometer. Take off the heat, pour over the gelatine mixture and mix well.

**4** Whisk the egg white in a large bowl with an electric whisk until stiff peaks form, then pour in the hot sugar syrup from the pan in a slow, steady stream, whisking all the time. The mixture becomes shiny and starts to thicken. Add the vanilla extract and continue whisking for 5–10 minutes until the mixture is stiff and thick. When you lift the beaters, a trail of the mixture should remain on the surface for 3 seconds.

**5** Spoon the mixture into the prepared star moulds and smooth with a wet palette knife. Leave to set for at least 1 hour in a cool place (but not in the refrigerator).

**6** Dust your work surface with more of the icing sugar-and-cornflour mixture. Loosen the marshmallows around the edges of each mould with a small knife, then turn them out onto the dusted surface. Decorate the marshmallows to your heart's content (try edible lustre sprays, available online, or melted chocolate with any sprinkles you fancy), then add them to your candy carousel (*see* pages 48–9) if you wish! Alternatively, store them in a lined airtight container, separating each marshmallow from the next with nonstick baking paper.

# Jammy Carousel Horses

MAKES 30
PREP 30 mins,
plus chilling and cooling
COOK 10 mins

160g (5¾oz) unsalted butter, softened

3 tbsp caster sugar

1 tsp vanilla extract

grated rind of ½ lemon

2 free-range egg yolks

210g (7½oz) plain flour, plus extra for dusting

5–10 tbsp raspberry or strawberry jam

**1** Cream the butter and sugar together with a wooden spoon or an electric whisk until light and fluffy. Beat in the vanilla extract, lemon rind and egg yolks, then finally mix in the flour.

**2** Wrap the dough in clingfilm and chill in the refrigerator for 30 minutes.

**3** Preheat the oven to 180°C/fan 160°C/gas mark 4. Line 3 baking sheets with nonstick baking paper.

**4** Remove the dough from the refrigerator and place it on a lightly floured work surface. Roll out the dough to a thickness of about 5mm (¼in).

**5** Cut 60 shapes from the dough using a horse-shaped cookie cutter and place them on the prepared baking sheets. Using a wooden skewer, give each horse a hole in the top of its back and another where its eye would be.

**6** Bake the dough shapes for 8–10 minutes until pale golden. Remove the baking sheets from the oven and allow them to stand for a few minutes, then transfer the cookies to wire racks to cool.

**7** When cool, spread ½–1 teaspoon of jam on half the horses, leaving a 1cm (½in) border around the edges. Top with the other halves so that jam pokes through the eye holes.

**8** Skewer through the holes on the horses' backs with cocktail sticks and arrange the horses on your candy carousel (*see* pages 48–9).

A party is not a party without jelly and ice cream. Everyone knows this. Personally, I'm not a fan of the type of jelly made from jelly cubes, but I love this fresh fruit jelly. It's healthy, colourful and even better when served in a Victorian-style sweetie jar with a big dollop of ice cream!

# Fresh Fruit Jelly with Ice Cream

**1** Place the gelatine in a saucepan and pour over the juice. Leave to stand for 5–10 minutes.

**2** Gently heat the saucepan over a low heat until the gelatine has dissolved; do not let it boil.

**3** Carefully pour the jelly into sweetie jars, serving dishes or decorative glasses, then place them in the refrigerator for at least 2 hours until set. Serve with ice cream.

SERVES **6**

PREP **20** mins,
plus setting

COOK **5** mins

1 × 12g (½oz) sachet powdered gelatine

500ml (18fl oz) fresh juice, such as orange, mango or passion fruit (avoid pineapple, papaya and kiwi, as they affect how the gelatine sets)

ice cream, to serve

I'm a bit embarrassed to admit this, but my father and I have a secret competition every year at my Auntie's house to see who can hide the greatest number of her butterfly cakes so that we can smuggle them home at the end. I'm particularly embarrassed, as I'm using the present tense! My Auntie's cakes are so yummy, and the entire family has loved them for as long as I can remember. These light and zesty bites are a real treat.

# ORANGE & LEMON BUTTERFLY CAKES

MAKES 20
PREP 20 mins
COOK 15 mins

**For the cake**

30g (1oz) unsalted butter, softened

90g (3¼oz) golden caster sugar

1 large free-range egg, beaten

100g (3½oz) self-raising flour

grated rind of 1 orange

grated rind of 1 lemon

60ml (2¼fl oz) milk

**For the buttercream icing**

100g (3½oz) unsalted butter, softened

100g (3½oz) icing sugar

**1** Preheat the oven to 180°C/fan 160°C/gas mark 4. Line 2 × 12-cup mini-muffin tins with 20 paper mini-muffin cases.

**2** To make the cake, cream the butter and sugar together with a wooden spoon or an electric whisk until light and fluffy. While you are still beating, add the egg and continue beating until thoroughly mixed.

**3** Beat in the flour and half the orange and lemon rind until just combined.

**4** Beat in the milk and spoon the mixture into the paper muffin cases. Bake in the middle of the oven for 15 minutes or until golden and risen.

**5** Remove from the oven and leave to cool in the tin on a wire rack.

**6** To make the buttercream icing, beat together the butter, icing sugar and the remaining orange and lemon rind using a wooden spoon or an electric whisk until smooth and creamy.

**7** When the cakes are cool, use a small serrated knife to carefully slice a small round from the top of each cake. Cut each round in half. Spoon a little icing on top of each cake, then gently replace the halved rounds in a butterfly-wing position.

This is the perfect way to dress up a banana, and it's speedy, too! Cream, toffee plus dark chocolate equals deliciousness. The only thing you will have to decide is what the bananas will wear. Hundreds and thousands, crushed pistachio nuts, sprinkles of any flavour... the list is endless.

# BANANA SPLITS

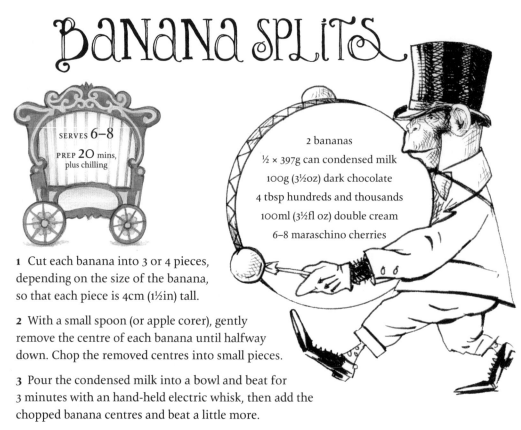

SERVES 6–8

PREP 20 mins,
plus chilling

2 bananas
½ × 397g can condensed milk
100g (3½oz) dark chocolate
4 tbsp hundreds and thousands
100ml (3½fl oz) double cream
6–8 maraschino cherries

1  Cut each banana into 3 or 4 pieces, depending on the size of the banana, so that each piece is 4cm (1½in) tall.

2  With a small spoon (or apple corer), gently remove the centre of each banana until halfway down. Chop the removed centres into small pieces.

3  Pour the condensed milk into a bowl and beat for 3 minutes with an hand-held electric whisk, then add the chopped banana centres and beat a little more.

4  Break the chocolate into pieces and melt it in a heatproof bowl set over a saucepan of barely simmering water, ensuring the base of the bowl doesn't touch the water below.

5  Pour the hundreds and thousands onto a saucer. Dip the bottom of each banana piece into the melted chocolate, then roll the chocolatey parts in the hundreds and thousands. Place the bananas, chocolate-end down, on some nonstick baking paper, spoon the banana-and-condensed milk mixture into the centres and leave to chill in the refrigerator for 1 hour.

6  Just before serving, whip up the cream and, using a star nozzle, pipe it on top of the bananas. Top each with a maraschino cherry.

I know a thing or two about moustaches. My dad had the best handlebar moustache in the 70s and 80s, and my partner has the biggest moustache in show business (or so he tells me)! So my moustache-shaped cookie cutters are treasured possessions.

# DOUBLE MILK CHOCOLATE MOUSTACHES

MAKES **16**

PREP **25** mins, plus chilling

COOK **15–20** mins

200g (7oz) unsalted butter, softened

150g (5½oz) caster sugar

1 free-range egg

250g (9oz) plain flour, plus extra for dusting

pinch of salt

2½ tbsp cocoa powder

100g (3½oz) milk chocolate chips, or a chocolate bar cut into small pieces

**1** Preheat the oven to 180°C/fan 160ºC/gas mark 4. Line a baking sheet with nonstick baking paper.

**2** Cream the butter and sugar together with a wooden spoon or an electric whisk until light and fluffy. Beat in the egg, then the flour, salt and cocoa powder. Fold in the chocolate chips or pieces, then bring the dough together in a ball. Wrap it in clingfilm and refrigerate for 20 minutes.

**3** Roll out the dough on a lightly floured work surface to a thickness of 5mm (¼in). Carefully cut out 16 shapes using a moustache-shaped cookie cutter (available online).

**4** Place the dough shapes on the baking sheet and bake for 15–20 minutes. Remove from the oven and cool on a wire rack.

Is anything
more beautiful
than a rainbow, with
its layers of rich colour,
one softly merging into the
next? To have this visual delight
in a teacup is a total treat, and a
refreshing one that will light up any
child's eyes and perk up their taste buds!

# RAINBOW SLUSHES

MAKES 6

PREP 10 mins,
plus freezing

12 ice lollies of varying colours

1 Remove the lollies from the freezer to defrost a little.
When they are slushy, pour a layer into 6 freezerpoof glasses;
put these in the freezer to set. Refrigerate the slushy lollies until
the first layer is frozen, then repeat the process until all the layers
are frozen. Place the slushes in the freezer until ready to serve.

What can be better on a warm summer's day than something sweet, cool and fizzy? There are no rules to devising your own combinations of soda and ice-cream flavours – make them as wacky or conventional as you like. As a kid I always had cola and vanilla ice cream. How do you float yours?

# ice-cream soda

MAKES **1**

PREP **1** min

200ml (¹/₃ pint) soda of your choice
(cola, lemonade or some other), chilled

1 scoop of ice cream

**1** Pour the soda into a tall glass.

**2** Top the soda with a scoop of ice cream and add a colourful straw.

## TIP

Line a baking sheet with nonstick baking paper and place this in the freezer until cool. Remove the ice cream from the freezer and allow it to stand until slightly softened. Then remove the prepared baking sheet from the freezer and place scoops of ice cream onto it as quickly as you can so that the ice-cream scoops don't melt. This will make things easier for you during a party, as all you need to do then is to pour your sodas and simply pop the prepared scoops into the drinks. No struggling with rock-solid ice cream and an unwieldy ice-cream scoop for the elegant hostess!

# How to Create
# Minnie-Mouse Ears

Minnie Mouse first shimmied onto the silver screen as Mickey Mouse's love interest in the 1928 film *Steamboat Willie*. With her red polka dots and oversized bow and shoes, Minnie is a classic childhood style icon, and recreating her famous mouse ears couldn't be easier! This hairstyle will work well on all hair types but, of course, it can't be done with hair that is any shorter than shoulder length, as short hair cannot be placed in a high bun.

**YOU WILL NEED**

hairbrush ✦ 2 hairbands ✦ tail comb ✦ bristle brush

hairspray ✦ hairpins ✦ 2 ribbons tied in a bow,

or a bow on a pin

◁ **STEP 1** Brush the hair and part it neatly into even ponytails, securing each with a hairband. Each ponytail should be positioned high on the head, where the "ears" will be.

◁ **STEP 2** Backcomb 1 ponytail with a tail comb, then gently smooth the surface of the hair with a bristle brush – take care not to brush out the volume you've just added. Now spray the ponytail with hairspray. Repeat with the other ponytail.

▷ **STEP 3** Holding the end of a ponytail, roll it forwards loosely, turning the hair over towards the front of the head. Hold the roll in place with 1 hand and use the other to fan out the hair so that the 2 sides of the roll sit on the head on either side of the roll. Pin the roll in place, then repeat on the other side. Smooth flyaway strands with your hand and spray the rolls with hairspray.

◁ **STEP 4** For the finishing touch, pin a bow to the base of each bun or between them. It's worth remembering that later, when the party is over and you are brushing out backcombed hair, you should always work from the ends of the hair and up the hairshaft, rather than downwards along it.

The 13th birthday is pretty significant for a young lady. It's a rite of passage into the next stage of your blossoming life. Thirteen opens the doors to experimentation – with make-up, cooking and dressing up, and in developing your passions – so it should be celebrated! My own obsession with car boot sales started at this age, which was considered odd for someone so young. Whatever your passion, follow your heart and do what you want to do – but do it well! You never know where it could lead…

When I was at school I had several best friends, and as soon as I was home from a long day at school I would call them and chat to them for hours. My dad just could not understand what we had to talk about, having been together at school all day long and, looking back, I have no idea either! I always used to nibble at cheese and fruit while I was on the phone, and this recipe is an updated, more elegant version of that snack, using soft creamy goats' cheese, rolled in anything you like.

# Goats' Cheese Truffles

MAKES 10

PREP 10 mins, plus chilling

300g (10½oz) goats' cheese, chilled

**Your choice of the following coatings (each yields enough mixture to coat about 10 truffles, depending on how thick you like your coating to be)**

2 tbsp chopped green herbs, such as chives, parsley or mint, plus a sprinkling of cracked black pepper

1 tbsp smoked sweet paprika

2 tbsp toasted sesame seeds

2 tbsp poppy seeds

2 tbsp chopped nuts, such as walnuts, pine nuts or pistachio nuts

2 tbsp finely chopped dried fruit, such as apricots

**1** Line a baking sheet with nonstick baking paper. Shape a small spoonful of goats' cheese about the size of a walnut into a ball by rolling it between the palms of your hands. Place it on the prepared baking sheet. Repeat with the remaining cheese until you have 10 balls.

**2** Put your chosen coatings on individual saucers and roll each truffle in the coating, ensuring it is evenly coated, then place it on the prepared baking sheet.

**3** Cover the truffles loosely with clingfilm and chill them in the refrigerator for 20 minutes.

**4** When you are ready to eat, pierce each truffle with a decorated cocktail stick (which makes it easier to pick up the truffles), then transfer them, one by one, onto a decorative serving dish.

I insisted that the theme of my coming-of-age party be mocktails and canapés because I wanted to be grown up, and had often seen my mum eat canapés at parties. My Rose Beef Bites are delicate and also delicious, as beef and horseradish are lifelong friends. Spending a tiny bit of time ensuring the beef looks pretty makes these canapés stunning to behold. Assemble the beef before the party, so then it's only a matter of spread, drop, serve and smile!

# Rose Beef Bites
## with Horseradish Cream

MAKES **18**

PREP **20** mins

COOK **7–10** mins

1 small baguette

30g (1oz) butter, melted

9 thin slices of rare roast beef

18 watercress leaves

**For the horseradish cream**

100ml (3½fl oz) crème fraîche

1 tbsp grated horseradish

salt and black pepper

**1** Preheat the oven to 180°C/fan 160°C/gas mark 4. Slice the baguette into 18 thin rounds. Brush both sides of each slice with melted butter. Place the baguette rounds on a baking sheet and toast them in the oven for about 7–10 minutes, turning halfway through, until brown, then allow to cool.

**2** To make the horseradish cream, combine the crème fraîche with the horseradish and season to taste. When the baguette rounds have cooled, place a spoonful of horseradish cream on top of each one.

**3** Cut each slice of beef in half lengthways, then roll it up to form a pretty rose spiral. Place a roll of beef on top of each baguette round, then garnish with watercress leaves.

At every party I threw during my teens my mum made chicken on sticks. She knew it was foolproof. The chicken was sometimes flavoured with barbecue sauce, sometimes with Mexican or Indian spices, and at other times it would be cooked on the barbecue with lots of vegetables. Below is my favourite variation; I loved the kick of the harissa, and the sweet pea and watercress soup is a fantastic complement. Serve the chicken on decorative cocktail sticks, which look incredibly feminine next to a teacup of soup.

# STICKY CHICKEN SKEWERS WITH PEA & WATERCRESS SOUP

SERVES 6

PREP 35 mins,
plus marinating
and cooling

COOK 20 mins

**For the skewers**

1 tbsp vegetable oil

1 tsp smoked sweet paprika

pinch of salt

1 skinless chicken breast, cut into thumbnail-sized pieces

1 tomato, deseeded and cut into thumbnail-sized pieces

1 tbsp harissa

**For the soup**

30g (1oz) butter

1 small onion, thinly sliced

150g (5½oz) watercress

500ml (18fl oz) chicken or vegetable stock

500g (1lb 2oz) fresh peas

small packet chervil, finely chopped

**1** To make the chicken skewers, mix the oil, paprika and salt together in a bowl, then add the chicken, coating it well. Cover the bowl with clingfilm and leave it in the refrigerator for 30 minutes to marinate.

**2** Heat a frying pan over a medium heat and fry the chicken for 5–7 minutes until cooked through, nudging it around to stop it sticking to the pan. Don't allow it to brown too much – it should remain moist. Set the chicken aside until it is cool enough to handle.

**3** To assemble the skewers, thread the chicken and tomato pieces onto decorative cocktail sticks and sprinkle with the harissa.

**4** To make the soup, melt the butter in a saucepan set over a medium heat. Add the onion and cook for 5–7 minutes until softened. Add the watercress and cook for a further 2–3 minutes until it wilts.

**5** Add the stock, peas and half the chervil. Bring to the boil, reduce the heat and simmer for 3–4 minutes until the peas are cooked.

**6** To prevent the soup from overcooking, pour it into a large bowl and sit it in a bowl of ice cubes. Allow the soup to cool completely, then purée it in a food processor and pass it through a fine sieve. Stir in the remaining chervil and serve the soup with the chicken skewers.

My obsession with Tarte Tatin will never end, and I hope by the time I'm 100 I will have tarte tatined everything possible! This is my newest elegant take on a favourite after-school treat – an onion sandwich. My mum often cooked onions as the base of dishes, and the wonderful smell of buttery, salted onions was too much to take! We often shared a naughty onion sandwich while talking about our days. I'm sure she always cooked extra onions to compensate.

MAKES **6**

PREP **25** mins

COOK **40** mins

# Shallot Tartes Tatin

5 shallots

30g (1oz) butter

1 tsp caster sugar

1 tsp thyme leaves

2 bay leaves

1 tbsp balsamic vinegar

100ml (3½fl oz) red wine

salt and black pepper

225g (8oz) shop-bought all-butter puff pastry

plain flour, for dusting

**1** Remove the skins from the shallots and cut them into quarters lengthways, cutting from the stem straight through the root.

**2** Heat the butter and sugar in a heavy-based saucepan set over a medium heat. When the butter begins to bubble, scatter in the thyme leaves and bay leaves, then add the shallots. Cook for 5 minutes, stirring occasionally. Pour over the balsamic vinegar and red wine, then season to taste. Reduce the heat and cook gently for 12–15 minutes.

**3** Meanwhile, preheat the oven to 190°C/fan 170°C/gas mark 5. Roll out the pastry on a lightly floured work surface to a thickness of 5mm (¼in). Make sure that you roll it out so that it is large enough to cut into 6 × 7cm (2¾in) rounds. Cut out the pastry rounds using a pastry cutter.

**4** Divide the shallots between 6 cups of a cupcake tin. Cover each with a disc of pastry and gently press it down around the edges. Bake the tarts for about 15–20 minutes until golden and puffed up. Serve the tarts immediately.

This Italian delight is a great sweet to add to your young lady's party. What could be better than a blend of almond, orange and chocolate? Biscotti are easy to eat, simple to prepare and can be made up to two weeks in advance. Then it's just a matter of getting them out of the tin to serve!

# Almond & Orange Biscotti

MAKES **12**

PREP **15** mins,
plus cooling

COOK **50** mins

100g (3½oz) plain flour, plus extra for dusting

1 tsp baking powder

pinch of salt

30g (1oz) butter, softened

70g (2½oz) granulated sugar

1 free-range egg

30g (1oz) chopped almonds

1 tsp freshly squeezed orange juice

grated rind of ½ orange

1 tsp orange liqueur

50g (1¾oz) white, milk or dark chocolate, broken into pieces, to decorate (optional)

**1** Preheat the oven to 180°C/fan 160°C/gas mark 4. Mix together the flour, baking powder and salt in a medium-sized bowl.

**2** Cream the butter and sugar together with a wooden spoon or an electric whisk until light and fluffy. Add the egg and beat until combined. Stir in the almonds, orange juice and rind and liqueur. Gradually add the flour mixture and mix until well combined.

**3** Line a baking sheet with nonstick baking paper and dust it lightly with flour. Turn out the dough on the sheet and shape it into a 8cm × 20cm (3¼in × 8in) flattened log.

**4** Bake the log for 30 minutes or until the dough is golden and firm to the touch. Allow to cool for at least 15 minutes. Cut the log at an angle into 12 × 1cm (½in) slices. Place these on the baking sheet and bake for 8 minutes, then turn and bake for 8 minutes until golden. Cool on a wire rack.

**5** If using, melt the chocolate in a heatproof bowl set over a saucepan of barely simmering water, ensuring the base of the bowl doesn't touch the water below. Allow to cool a little, then transfer to a piping bag. Decorate the biscotti by piping the chocolate over them.

Two delicacies dancing together on a sea of lace... One will take you moments to prepare; the other will require patience and practice. Both are bites of melodious heaven and will have your young ladies pirouetting to the table again and again.

# COCONUT ICE SQUARES

**MAKES 24**

PREP **10** mins, plus chilling

397g can condensed milk

500g (1lb 2oz) icing sugar, sifted

300g (10½oz) desiccated coconut

few drops of pink or red food colouring

**1** Line a 20cm (8in) square loose-bottomed cake tin with nonstick baking paper.

**2** Mix together the milk and icing sugar in a large bowl. Add the desiccated coconut gradually until the mixture is firm but not crumbling apart. To test, take a walnut-sized ball of the mixture and press it in the palm of your hand. If it holds its shape, it's ready, but if it sags or is very sticky, add more coconut.

**3** Press half the mixture into the prepared cake tin. Mix a few drops of food colouring into the remaining half of the mixture and work the colour through thoroughly, then press the coloured mixture on top of the white layer in the cake tin. Chill the mixture in the refrigerator for 2 hours to allow it to harden.

**4** Cut the coconut ice into 24 squares to serve.

# CHOCOLATE MACAROONS WITH PEARLS

MAKES **15–20**

PREP **25** mins, plus setting

COOK **7–8** mins

**For the macaroons**

70g (2½oz) ground almonds

140g (5oz) icing sugar

15g (½oz) cocoa powder

2 free-range egg whites, beaten until stiff peaks form

**For the filling**

75ml (2½fl oz) whipping cream

70g (2½oz) mascarpone cheese

30g (1oz) icing sugar

seeds from 1 vanilla pod

50g (1¾oz) edible pearls (available online)

**1** Preheat the oven to 180°C/fan 160°C/gas mark 4. Line a baking sheet with nonstick baking paper.

**2** For the macaroons, mix the almonds, icing sugar and cocoa powder in a bowl. Fold in the egg whites. Transfer to a piping bag and pipe 15–20 × 3cm (1¼in) rounds onto the baking sheet. Allow to set for 15 minutes, then bake for 7–8 minutes, with the oven door slightly ajar.

**3** To remove the macaroons from the paper without them sticking, lift 1 corner of the paper and pour some boiled water onto the baking sheet. As water hits the underside of the paper, the macaroons lift off easily.

**4** To make the filling, whisk the cream, mascarpone, icing sugar and vanilla seeds together in a bowl. Spoon the mixture into a piping bag fitted with a 1cm (½in) plain nozzle. Line up the macaroons in 2 lines. Pipe a generous dollop of cream onto half of them, then top each with an uncovered one and press gently.

**5** Place the edible pearls on a large plate and gently roll the filled macaroons through them to cover the sides with the pearls.

At every party there must be a dish that whisks you off on a fairy-tale journey to a place where only you and the pudding will live happily ever after. These tartlets capture this moment perfectly. Pear and chocolate are natural bedfellows, and the mint adds a fantastic burst of freshness.

# Pear & Mint Chocolate Tartlets

MAKES 6

PREP 40 mins,
plus marinating and chilling

COOK 40–50 mins

1 vanilla pod

1 bottle of red wine

225g (8oz) caster sugar

1 cinnamon stick, snapped
in half

few sprigs of mint

4 pears, peeled but kept whole

**For the chocolate ganache**

100g (3½oz) dark chocolate,
broken into pieces

100ml (3½fl oz) double cream

30g (1oz) mint

15g (½oz) butter

**For the pastry**

50g (1¾oz) icing sugar

35g (1¼oz) cocoa powder

100g (3½oz) plain flour, plus extra
for dusting

65g (2¼oz) butter, chilled

1 free-range egg yolk

**1** Halve the vanilla pod lengthways, scrape out the black seeds and put them in a large saucepan with the wine, sugar, cinnamon and mint. Cut each piece of pod into 3 long thin strips and add these to pan, then lower the pears into the pan.

**2** Poach the pears, covered, for about 20–30 minutes, depending on their ripeness – once cooked, they should be tender all the way through when pierced with a cocktail stick. (Try not to overcook them, as this will make slicing them difficult later on.) Allow the pears to cool in the wine and leave them to marinate for at least 3 hours, or overnight, to soak up the colour.

**3** For the ganache, put the chocolate in a heatproof bowl. Heat the cream and mint in a small saucepan until bubbles form at the edges. Strain the cream, pouring it onto the chocolate. Stir until the chocolate melts and combines with the cream, then add the butter and stir again. Allow the mixture to cool, then chill in the refrigerator for 30–60 minutes.

**4** To make the pastry, combine the icing sugar, cocoa powder and flour in a large bowl. Cut the butter into small cubes and rub it into the dry ingredients with your fingertips until the mixture resembles breadcrumbs. Add the egg yolk and combine. The mixture should form a ball, but if it is still dry and crumbly, slowly add up to 1 tablespoon iced water, ensuring the mixture does not get too wet. Wrap the dough with clingfilm and chill in the refrigerator for about 30 minutes.

**5** Preheat the oven to 160°C/fan 140°C/gas mark 3. Roll out the dough on a lightly floured work surface to a thickness of 3mm (⅛in) and cut out 6 × 14cm- (5½in-) diameter discs. Press the discs into 6 × 9cm- (3½in-) diameter tartlet cases. Trim any overlapping dough to neaten. Cut out discs of nonstick paper, place these on the dough, then put baking beans on top. Bake for 10 minutes. Remove the paper and beans and bake for a few more minutes until the pastry has hardened, then leave to cool.

**6** Unmould and fill the pastry cases with the ganache. (If it is still soft, refrigerate the tartlets for an hour or so until firm.) Slice the pears in half lengthways, then cut them into thin slices. Arrange on top of each tartlet in a rose shape, using the picture opposite as a guide.

No party for a young lady is complete without the all-important mocktail! The two recipes given here are my personal favourites, but I insist you tailor them to your own taste. The excitement is in the making and experimenting. I had a pink cocktail maker in my teenage years, and I loved mixing fruits, balancing flavours and making things fizz. So cheers, my beautiful young dears! May your teenage years be full of happiness.

# MOCKTAILS

## VIRGIN STRAWBERRY DAIQUIRI

SERVES 6

PREP 2 mins

100g (3½oz) frozen strawberries

pinch of salt

1 tsp caster sugar

4 ice cubes

**1** Place the strawberries, salt, sugar and ice cubes in a blender and blend the concoction until smooth. Serve chilled, in grown-up cocktail glasses.

## VIRGIN APPLE FIZZ

SERVES 6

PREP 2 mins

125ml (4fl oz) apple juice

½ tsp lemon juice

1 tsp sugar syrup

crushed ice

sparkling water or lemonade

**1** Put the juices and sugar syrup in a cocktail shaker with crushed ice and shake for 5–10 seconds. Strain the mixture into 6 glasses, then fill the rest of each glass with sparkling water or lemonade.

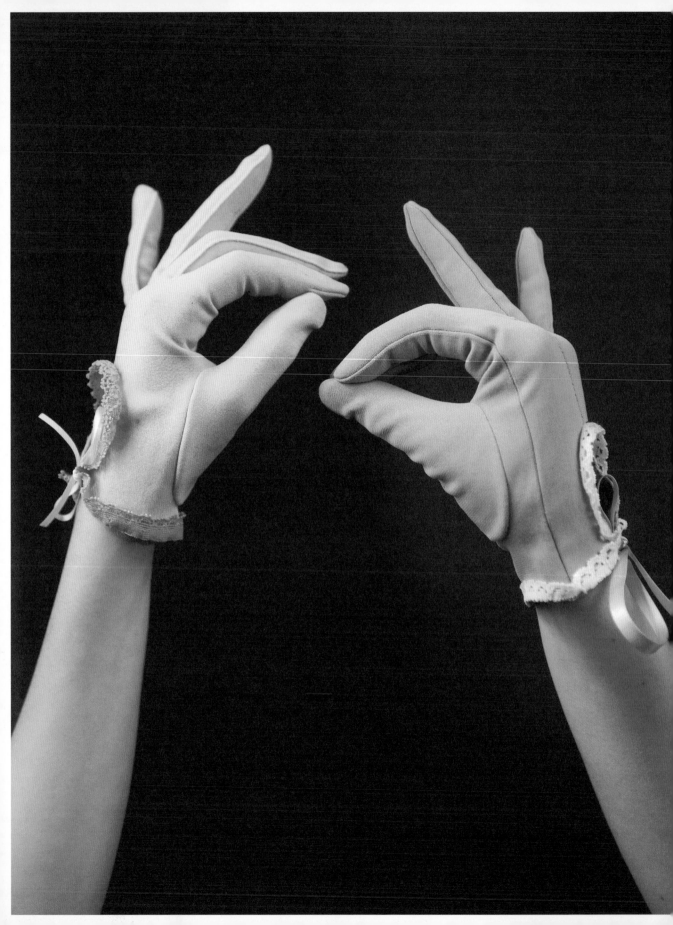

# How to Make
# Elegant Cut-out
# Gloves

What should a chic young woman wear to her coming of age party? Elegant gloves, of course! You can show these off as you daintily eat and drink the splendid delicacies on offer. And the best bit? When asked where you got them from, you can mention how you customized them, so they are the only pair like this in the whole world!

### YOU WILL NEED

✄ pair of fabric gloves (not knitted, suede or leather) ✄ thin marker pen

✄ fabric scissors ✄ 1m (1yd) pretty elastic lace ✄ needle and thread

to match the colour of your gloves ✄ 50cm (½yd) thin ribbon

in a shade that complements the colour of your gloves

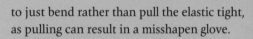

1 Put on 1 glove and, using your other hand and a thin marker pen, draw a teardrop shape on the back of your hand where you would like the cut-out section to be. Start off small – you can always make it larger if you want to. When you are happy with the shape, cut it out, and use it as a template to cut out exactly the same shape on the second glove.

2 Now attach the elastic lace to the cuff and cut-out section of each glove. Begin at a side seam, with the bottom edge of the elastic in line with the cuff. Use a small blanket stitch to join the 2 together, easing the elastic around the curve of the cut-out section. Try

to just bend rather than pull the elastic tight, as pulling can result in a misshapen glove.

3 When you have sewn the elastic on all the way around the base of the glove, cut off any remaining elastic. Use a couple of stitches to join the ends of the elastic neatly.

4 Now cut 2 pieces of ribbon, each 10cm (4in) long, and sew 1 to the wrong side of the glove fabric at each side of the base of your teardrop shape, at the cuff. When finished, tie the ribbon into a pretty bow.

5 Repeat this process on the other glove to complete the pair.

# HOW TO CREATE THE
## Hair Bow

It was only in the 1950s that the word "teenager" was created; before then, young ladies were expected to be little adults in training and were taught the finer details of how to take care of a household. Playing grown-ups can certainly be fun, and this hair-do is sophisticated, yet very clearly shouts "I'm still a teenager!"

### YOU WILL NEED

⮑ hairband ⮑ bristle brush ⮑ hairspray ⮑ section clips and hairpins ⮑ tail comb

◁ **STEP 1** Gather your hair into a ponytail at the top of the head and secure it with a hairband, ensuring that any flyaway strands are smoothed and sprayed into place. (If the ponytail is not sitting on the top of the head, the "bow" will not be upright.)

◁ **STEP 3** Take 1 of the 2 outer sections of hair and backcomb its entire length. Spray this backcombed section of hair liberally with hairspray and smooth the hair gently with a bristle brush.

▷ **STEP 2** Divide the ponytail into 3 even sections. Use a section clip to hold each section of the ponytail separately.

▷ **STEP 4** Pull the backcombed section horizontally and fold the hair in half. Bring the ends of this section to the base of the ponytail, creating 1 half of the bow. Secure it with hairpins. Repeat steps 3 and 4 with the other outer section of the ponytail, creating the other half of the bow. Leave the middle section clipped out of the way.

◁ **STEP 5** Take the middle section of hair and wrap it over the front of the ponytail to cover the hairband, then divide the hair to wind each section underneath each side of the bow. How many times you wrap the hair around the bow will depend on the length of the hair, but try to create a neat vertical fold of hair, which produces the bow effect.

▷ **STEP 6** Use hairpins to secure the base of the bow.

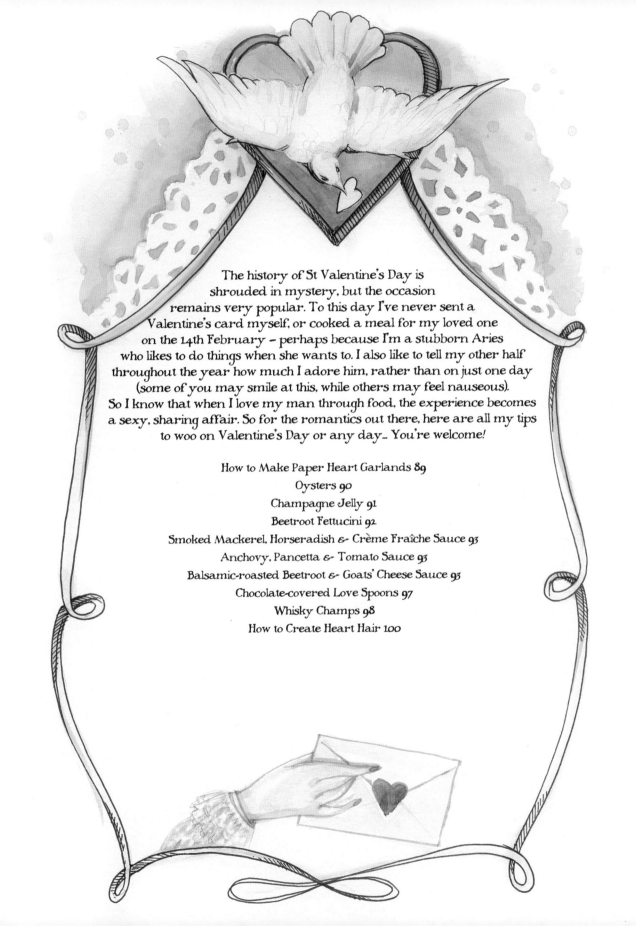

The history of St Valentine's Day is
shrouded in mystery, but the occasion
remains very popular. To this day I've never sent a
Valentine's card myself, or cooked a meal for my loved one
on the 14th February – perhaps because I'm a stubborn Aries
who likes to do things when she wants to. I also like to tell my other half
throughout the year how much I adore him, rather than on just one day
(some of you may smile at this, while others may feel nauseous).
So I know that when I love my man through food, the experience becomes
a sexy, sharing affair. So for the romantics out there, here are all my tips
to woo on Valentine's Day or any day... You're welcome!

# HOW TO MAKE PAPER HEART GARLANDS

Giving your heart away has never been so much fun! Collect maps, receipts, postcards and any other scraps of paper from places you and your Valentine have visited to give your paper heart sentiment and meaning. One heart is all you need, but why stop there? Show off! Hang garlands from the ceiling and around the table, and welcome your partner into the love cave! Cheesy? Hell, yeah!

**YOU WILL NEED**

♡ maps, receipts, postcards or other paper to make the hearts ♡ paper scissors

♡ stapler ♡ ribbon – cut the length you want your garlands to hang

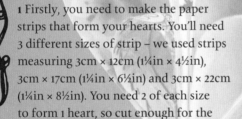
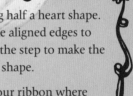

1 Firstly, you need to make the paper strips that form your hearts. You'll need 3 different sizes of strip – we used strips measuring 3cm × 12cm (1¼in × 4½in), 3cm × 17cm (1¼in × 6½in) and 3cm × 22cm (1¼in × 8½in). You need 2 of each size to form 1 heart, so cut enough for the number of hearts you want to make.

2 Take 1 strip of each size and lay these on top of each other so that they are lined up along 1 of the 3cm (1¼in) edges. Hold them together along the bottom and, one by one, bend the other 3cm (1¼in) edges over to line up with the aligned edges. All the 3cm (1¼in) edges should now be

held together, creating half a heart shape. Staple this shape at the aligned edges to secure it. Now repeat the step to make the second half of a heart shape.

3 Find the point on your ribbon where you want your hearts to start. Line up your 2 heart halves on either side of the ribbon so that the ribbon runs between them, then staple the paper in place.

4 Repeat the previous steps as many times as you like, filling your hanging garland with hearts. Or make just a single heart to hang as a decoration.

# OYSTERS

**SERVES 2**
**PREP 10–15 mins**

100g (3½oz) raspberries

50ml (2fl oz) red wine vinegar

1 shallot, finely chopped

1 tsp black pepper

pinch of flaked sea salt

12 chilled fresh oysters

crushed ice

rock salt, to serve

**1** Press the raspberries through a sieve with a wooden spoon or a rubber spatula to remove the seeds. Discard the seeds.

**2** In a small bowl, combine the raspberry purée with the red wine vinegar, shallot and pepper. Season with the salt.

**3** Shuck and loosen the oysters from their shells, but leave them in their shells for ease of eating. Store the oysters on crushed ice.

**4** Spoon about 1 teaspoon of the raspberry vinegar onto each oyster and serve on a bed of rock salt.

The beauty of jelly is in the gentle wobble of the set. Any vessel can showcase this refreshing palate-cleanser. I love the classic combination of strawberries with Champagne, but use any berry you fancy and be creative with what you serve it in.

# CHAMPAGNE JELLY

SERVES **2**

PREP **15** mins, plus chilling

COOK **5** mins

½ × 12g (½ oz) sachet gelatine
250ml (9fl oz) Champagne
2 strawberries, sliced

**1** Place the gelatine in a saucepan and pour over the Champagne. Allow to stand for 5 minutes, then place the mixture over a low heat and slowly allow the gelatine to dissolve, occasionally stirring gently with a spatula. Do not allow the mixture to boil. Once the gelatine has dissolved, take the pan off the heat and allow to cool a little.

**2** Divide the Champagne between 2 small heart-shaped ramekins or pretty dishes. Tap the dishes firmly on the work surface to release any air bubbles. Place a few strawberry slices in each dish. Refrigerate for 1–1½ hours until the jellies are firm.

Food made with love tastes better – fact. Give yourself time to prepare this dish, especially if this is your first time making pasta, and ensure you get the best-quality pasta flour you can; it really makes a difference. With the hard work done and your amazing, earthy pasta in the pan, show off a bit more by creating three simple but delicious pasta sauces. Your other half will be spinning with excitement and won't know where to put his fork first!

# Beetroot Fettucini

SERVES 2

PREP 30 mins, plus resting

COOK 10 mins

300g (10½oz) "00" flour or pasta flour, plus extra for dusting

2 free-range eggs and 1 free-range egg yolk

salt

75g (2¾oz) cooked beetroot, puréed

**1** Place the flour in a mound in the centre of a large work surface and make a well in the middle. Pour the eggs and egg yolk into the well and add a pinch of salt and 2 large tablespoons of the puréed beetroot.

**2** Using a fork, beat the egg mixture, slowly incorporating the flour, beginning at the inner rim of the well. When the flour is incorporated, gather the dough together to form a rounded mass. Begin kneading the dough with the palms of your hands. If it seems too stiff, add a little more of the puréed beetroot. If it seems too sticky, add more flour.

**3** Knead the dough on a lightly floured work surface for 5–10 minutes until it is smooth and elastic. Wrap the dough in clingfilm, place it in a bowl and let it rest for 30 minutes at room temperature.

**4** Divide the dough into 8 equal pieces and pat them flat. Lightly flour the pieces and cover them with clingfilm until you are ready to press them. Pass the first piece through the widest setting of your pasta machine twice, each time folding it in half before rolling it through again. Continue rolling the dough in this way, setting the machine 1 step smaller and passing the dough through twice on each setting.

**5** Attach the pasta cutter to the machine and run the lengths of dough through it. Lightly coat the fettucini with flour and let it rest, or hang it up in strips for roughly 10 minutes to dry.

**6** Bring a large saucepan of salted water to the boil. Add the remaining beetroot to the pasta water. Add the pasta and cook for 3 minutes. Drain and serve a third of the pasta with each of the individual sauces.

# SMOKED MACKEREL,
## HORSERADISH & CRÈME FRAÎCHE SAUCE

PREP **5** mins

COOK **10** mins

1 tbsp olive oil

1 shallot, chopped

75ml (2½fl oz) white wine

125ml (4fl oz) crème fraîche

1 tbsp horseradish sauce

grated rind and juice of ½ lemon

100g (3½oz) smoked mackerel, flaked

salt and black pepper

chopped dill, to garnish

**1** Heat the oil in a frying pan set over a medium heat. Add the shallot and fry until softened.

**2** Add the white wine. Bring the mixture to the boil and simmer for about 5 minutes until the liquid volume is reduced by half.

**3** Add the crème fraîche, horseradish sauce, lemon rind and juice, flaked mackerel and seasoning and stir well to combine.

**4** Allow the sauce to warm through, then take it off the heat, add the cooked pasta and toss together. Serve immediately, garnished with dill.

# ANCHOVY, PANCETTA
## & TOMATO sauce

PREP **5** mins

COOK **15** mins

50g (1¾oz) pancetta, finely diced

½ shallot, finely diced

125ml (4fl oz) red wine

100g (3½oz) tomatoes, chopped

1 tbsp chopped parsley

4 anchovy fillets in oil, drained and roughly chopped

½ tbsp chopped capers

**1** Dry-fry the pancetta over a gentle heat.

**2** Add the shallot and cook it in the fat released from the pancetta until it has softened.

**3** Add the wine, chopped tomatoes, parsley, anchovy fillets and capers, then simmer the sauce for 10 minutes.

**4** Take the sauce off the heat, add the cooked pasta and toss together. Serve immediately.

# BALSAMIC-ROASTED BEETROOT
## & GOATS' CHEESE sauce

PREP **5** mins

COOK **1** hour

2 beetroot, peeled and quartered

2 tbsp olive oil

1 tbsp balsamic vinegar

1 small red onion, finely chopped

leaves from 2 sprigs of thyme

100ml (3½fl oz) crème fraîche

50g (1¾oz) goats' cheese, chopped into small pieces

Parmesan cheese, to serve

**1** Preheat the oven to 200°C/fan 180°C/gas mark 6. Toss the beetroot in half the oil and vinegar. Place the beetroot in a roasting tin and roast for about 45 minutes until cooked through.

**2** Meanwhile, heat the remaining oil and vinegar in a pan and fry the onion until softened. Add the thyme leaves. Transfer the beetroot to the pan, then add the crème fraîche. Simmer over a low heat until the crème fraîche is runny and the sauce is pink. Add the goats' cheese.

**3** Remove the sauce from the heat, add the cooked pasta and toss together. Serve immediately with some grated Parmesan.

Anchovy, Pancetta & Tomato Pasta Sauce

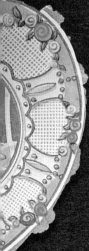

It's been proven that eating chocolate triggers the release of the happy hormone serotonin, promoting feelings of pleasure. So this chapter on love simply would not be complete without a lick of this good stuff. These love spoons are the grown-up version of a lollipop, and each time I make them I vary the flavours slightly to keep them interesting. So my man never knows exactly what he's putting in his mouth!

# CHOCOLATE-COVERED LOVE SPOONS

MAKES **4**

PREP **15** mins,
plus chilling

COOK **5** mins

75g (2¾oz) dark chocolate
1 tbsp brandy
pinch of chilli powder
¼ tsp ground cinnamon
pinch of ground nutmeg

**1** Break the chocolate into pieces and melt it in a heatproof bowl set over a saucepan of barely simmering water, ensuring the base of the bowl doesn't touch the water below. Reserve 3 tablespoons of melted chocolate in another bowl for coating.

**2** In a bowl, combine the brandy and spices with the melted chocolate. Fill the bowls of 4 ornate spoons with the melted-chocolate mixture, then set them on a tray and place them in the refrigerator for 10 minutes to allow the chocolate to harden a little.

**3** Remove the spoons from the refrigerator and coat them with the remaining melted chocolate. Allow to chill once more until hard.

**4** Serve the spoons with hot after-dinner drinks.

I may have mentioned before that my favourite drink is Champagne. But as a giving and sharing girlfriend, I don't like to be too selfish, so I've incorporated my man's favourite drink, whisky, in this recipe. The two are a match made in heaven!

# WHISKY CHAMPS

SERVES 2

PREP 5 mins

50ml (2fl oz) whisky

15ml (½fl oz) crème de frambois

200ml (1/3 pint) Champagne or sparkling wine

**1** If you're planning to serve this cocktail in a "love cup", as we have done, simply pour the whisky and crème de frambois into the cup and top up with bubbly, then share with your loved one. Alternatively, divide the whisky and the crème de frambois between 2 Champagne flutes, then fill to the top of the flutes with bubbly.

# HOW TO CREATE
# HEART HAIR

Why stop at food to show your love? With this cheeky hair-do you can wear your heart just a bit north of your sleeve, and remind your man that you love him with every bit of you – mind, body, soul... and hair!

## YOU WILL NEED

hair mousse ❧ tail comb ❧ curling tongs ❧ Kirby grips, curl clips (optional) and hairpins ❧ section clips ❧ hairspray ❧ bristle brush

### HOW TO CURL AND SET

The first step with most vintage hairstyles is to curl and set the hair.

To do this, apply some mousse liberally through the length of your hair and comb it through.

Taking sections of no more than 1cm (½in), curl the hair horizontally using your curling tongs and secure into pin curls with Kirby grips or curl clips.

If you don't have the time to sleep in your set and have decided to style it on the day, just leave your hair to cool for about 15–20 minutes.

▽ **STEP 1** After you have curled and set your hair (*see* box, left), part your hair using a tail comb into your desired parting. A central parting is recommended for symmetry with the heart-shaped victory rolls. Divide the hair into 4 sections by parting it from front to back and across the top of the head, from ear to ear. Secure the sections with section clips.

▷ **STEP 2** Position Kirby grips in a vertical line about 5cm (2in) away from the central parting on either side. Ensuring the grips overlap slightly provides a tighter, more secure hairstyle.

◁ **STEP 3** Lightly backcomb one of the back sections of hair with your tail comb and spray with hairspray. Taking a bristle brush, smooth this section of hair gently from the nape of the neck upwards.

◁ **STEP 5** Repeat step 4 on the other back section of hair. Ensure these 2 back victory rolls are of a similar size, in order to produce a symmetrical heart shape.

▷ **STEP 4** Roll 1 back section while pinching the ends of the hair under the roll, sweeping the roll towards the parting. Once you have your desired shape, use hairpins to hold it in place.

◁ **STEP 6** Now work on 1 of the front sections of hair. Backcomb and smooth it gently with a bristle brush. Form a victory roll at the front, ensuring it is in line with the back roll, and secure it with hairpins. Repeat this step with the other front section of hair. Next, carefully connect the top of 1 of the back rolls and the back of its corresponding front victory roll, using hairpins to make the join seamless. Repeat on the other side. Spray liberally with hairspray, using the palm of your hand to smooth over any stray hairs.

HEN TEA PARTY

Angel: "Hello, welcome to The Vintage Patisserie."

Customer: "Hello, I would like to enquire about a stylish hen party that my friends will love as well as my mum and my gran!"

Angel: "Fabulous, my dear, you have come to exactly the right place."

A staggering 75 per cent of our tea parties are for fervent brides-to-be, all of them with the same objectives in mind: fun, laughter, naughtiness and elegance. I'm pretty sure I've got this covered for you, so all you need to think about is how to tackle your hangover!

My continued obsession with anything edibly "rose" was the inspiration for this dish. The spicy kofta bites kick off a party in your mouth, while the refreshing and aromatic rose jelly lifts and refreshes your palate – allowing you to pop in that extra kofta and head right back to the party!

# Lamb Kofta with Rose jelly

SERVES **12**

PREP **15** mins, plus cooling/chilling

COOK **15** mins

**For the rose jelly**

200g (7oz) caster sugar

1 × 12g (½oz) sachet gelatine

2 tbsp rosewater

1 tbsp edible dried rose petals (available online)

**1** Heat the sugar with 500ml (18fl oz) water in a saucepan over a medium heat until the sugar has melted. Allow the syrup to cool, then add the gelatine and rosewater and leave to sit for 5 minutes. Heat the pan gently until the gelatine dissolves – do not let it boil. Remove the jelly from the heat and pour it into 12 shot glasses, sprinkle with the rose petals and leave in the refrigerator to set.

**For the koftas**

200g (7oz) lamb, minced

¼ small onion, chopped

30g (1oz) fresh white breadcrumbs

15g (½oz) parsley, chopped

5g (1/8oz) mint, chopped

1 garlic clove, finely chopped

¼ tsp ground cumin

¼ tsp ground cinnamon

¼ tsp ground ginger

¼ tsp salt

pinch of black pepper

2 tsp harissa

1 large free-range egg

sunflower oil, for shallow-frying

**1** Mix together all the ingredients except the oil in a large bowl with your hands. Shape the mixture into 24 small balls, set them on a plate, cover them with clingfilm and chill in the refrigerator for 30 minutes.

**2** Heat a little oil in a frying pan over a medium heat. Shallow-fry the koftas for about 5 minutes until golden and cooked through, then drain on kitchen paper. Skewer them with cocktail sticks and place 1 on top of each rose jelly shot glass. Place the extra koftas on a plate, for seconds.

When you are organizing the hen do of a dear friend, there have to be one or two dishes that satisfy the soul and are simple to prepare. I think of this favourite as a fancy pizza: crisp, juicy and full of flavour! In fact, don't be tied down to this recipe – your only limitation is what's in the fridge!

# RATATOUILLE TART

SERVES **6**

PREP **20** mins

COOK
**25–30** mins

1 courgette

1 aubergine

1 red pepper

250g (9oz) shop-bought all-butter
puff pastry

plain flour, for dusting

3 tbsp passata

2 tbsp extra-virgin olive oil

salt and black pepper

1 free-range egg, beaten, or milk, to glaze

leaves from 2 sprigs of basil

1 tbsp grated Parmesan cheese (optional)

**1** Preheat the oven to 180°C/fan 160ºC/gas mark 4.

**2** Line a large baking sheet with nonstick baking paper. Slice the courgette, aubergine and pepper into 2mm- ($^1/_{16}$in-) thick rings.

**3** Roll out the pastry dough on a lightly floured work surface to an 18cm × 30cm (7in × 12in) rectangle, neatening the edges with a long sharp knife. Lightly score a 2cm (¾in) border around the edges of the dough and gently pierce inside the border with a fork.

**4** Spread the dough with the passata, then layer the vegetables in alternating rows on top. Drizzle the vegetables with 1 tablespoon of the olive oil, and season generously. Brush the edges of the pastry with the egg or milk.

**5** Bake the tart for 25–30 minutes or until the vegetables are softened and the pastry is cooked through, risen and golden. Remove from the oven; sprinkle with the basil, the 1 tablespoon olive oil and Parmesan, if using.

When you're giggling and chattering away with your wonderful girlfriends, what could be better than popping a perfectly formed bite-sized piece of tastiness into your mouth? These filling little delights really do explode in the mouth and hit the spot and, what's better, is that they give you one hand free to… well, drink! For your vegetarian girlfriends, swap the pork for their favourite cheese-and-onion mixture.

# Rice Balls

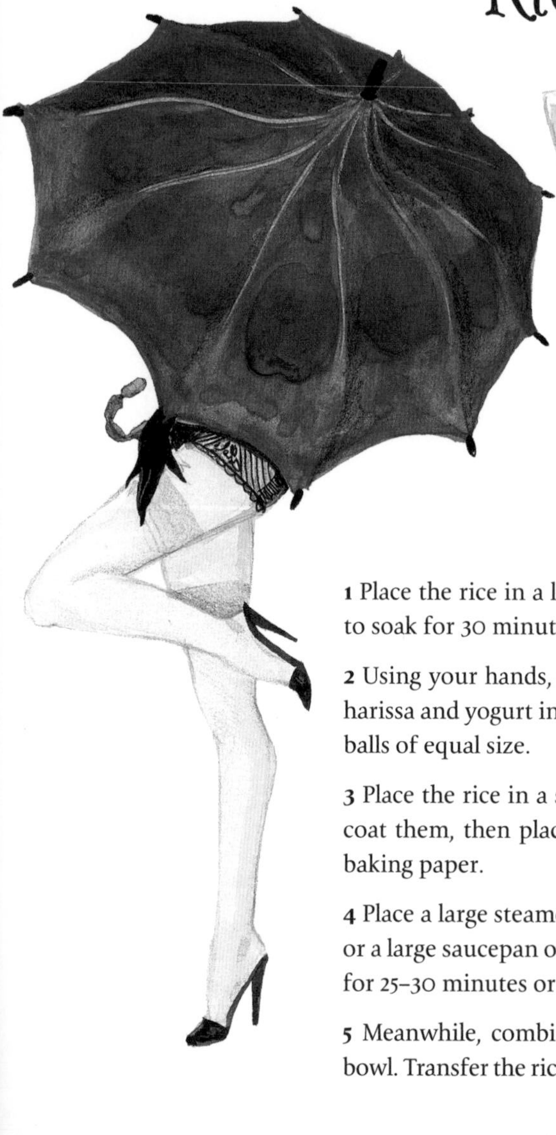

SERVES 6
PREP 15 mins, plus soaking
COOK 25–30 mins

210g (7½oz) basmati rice
500g (1lb 2oz) minced pork
1 tbsp plain flour
2 tsp ras el hanout
½ onion, diced
½ small carrot, peeled and grated
2 tbsp flaked almonds
50g (1¾oz) dried apricots, chopped
2 tbsp chopped coriander
1 tsp–1 tbsp harissa
100ml (3½fl oz) natural yogurt

1 Place the rice in a large bowl, cover it with cold water and leave it to soak for 30 minutes. Drain the rice well.

2 Using your hands, combine the remaining ingredients except the harissa and yogurt in a separate bowl, then shape the mixture into 12 balls of equal size.

3 Place the rice in a shallow dish. Roll the mince balls in the rice to coat them, then place them on a baking sheet lined with nonstick baking paper.

4 Place a large steamer lined with nonstick baking paper over a wok or a large saucepan of simmering water. Cook the rice balls, covered, for 25–30 minutes or until cooked through.

5 Meanwhile, combine the harissa (to taste) and yogurt in a small bowl. Transfer the rice balls to a plate and serve with the harissa sauce.

Originally from the Philippines, the sweet potato has become quite a favourite of us Brits. Personally, I like to "crisp, salt and eat" these flavoursome bites, and they are the perfect accompaniment for everything! Be careful, though – they may make you a little thirsty, so you might have to drink another cocktail to quench your thirst. Oh, it's a hard life!

# Sweet Potato Chips

SERVES 8
PREP 15 mins
COOK 15 mins

2 tsp sea salt flakes
½ tsp black pepper
½ tsp sweet paprika
½ tsp finely grated lemon rind
2 medium sweet potatoes, peeled
vegetable oil, for deep-frying

**1** Combine the salt, pepper, paprika and lemon rind in a frying pan over a low heat. Cook, stirring, for 1 minute or until fragrant. Remove the mixture from the heat and set it aside.

**2** Use a vegetable peeler to cut the sweet potatoes into long, thin ribbons. Place these on a tray lined with kitchen paper.

**3** Heat 10cm (4in) oil over a medium-high heat to 180°C (356°F). (When the oil is hot enough, a cube of bread dropped into it will turn golden brown in 15 seconds.)

**4** Deep-fry handfuls of the chips for 30 seconds or until golden, stirring gently with a slotted spoon so that they don't stick to the pan. Transfer the cooked chips to the prepared tray, and season with the salt mixture. Repeat the process with the remaining sweet potato and salt mixture. Serve immediately, or store the chips in an airtight container for a few days.

These little bites earn their ranking as one of the sweetest, smokiest, saltiest and most scrumptious party snacks in this book purely on name alone! There is a similar version that's made using oysters, called "Angels on Horseback" and, yes, that's exactly how I plan to be transported home when my Prince Charming comes to pick me up at the end of my hen do!

# Date Devils on Horseback

MAKES **24**

PREP **20** mins

COOK **10–15** mins

125g (4½oz) smoked almond kernels

60g (2¼oz) butter, at room temperature

24 pitted Medjool dates

6 thin rashers of rindless bacon

**1** Preheat the oven to 180°C/fan 160°C/gas mark 4. Process the almonds in a food processor until they are coarsely chopped. Add the butter and process again until it is well combined with the almonds. Divide the mixture evenly between the date cavities.

**2** Cut each rasher of bacon crossways into 4 pieces. Wrap a piece of bacon around each date. Skewer each bite with a cocktail stick.

**3** Place the bites on a baking sheet and bake them for about 10–15 minutes or until the bacon is cooked and the stuffing is heated through.

A mischievous ladies' gathering is incomplete without sweetness of the edible kind. These three cherry-picked delights will complement the night with a kiss. Pop a Maraschino Cookie to fuel some dance moves, or a Raspberry Custard Tart for a sweet-sharp taste sensation, or lose yourself in a Red Velvet Layer Cake. I challenge anyone not to feel seduced after these.

# Raspberry Custard Tarts

**MAKES 24**

PREP 30 mins, plus chilling and infusing

COOK 25 mins

250g (9oz) shop-bought sweet shortcrust pastry

24 raspberries

icing sugar, for dusting (optional)

**For the crème patissière**

1 vanilla pod, split lengthways

125ml (4fl oz) milk

1 free-range egg yolk

1 tbsp plain flour, plus extra for dusting

2 tbsp caster sugar

2 tbsp thick cream

**1** To make the tarts, roll out the pastry on a work surface dusted with flour to a thickness of about 1cm (½in). Using a pastry cutter, stamp out 24 discs, just larger than the cups of your mini-muffin tin (you may need to reroll the trimmings to get enough dough). Gently press a disc into each of the cups of 2 × 12-cup mini-muffin tins and prick the base of each pastry case with a fork. Lay a sheet of clingfilm over the pastry and fill each pastry case with baking beans. Place the muffin tins in the refrigerator to chill for 20 minutes. Preheat the oven to 190°C/fan 170°C/gas mark 5.

**2** Bake the cases for 10 minutes, then carefully remove the clingfilm and baking beans and bake for a further 3–5 minutes until the pastry has set and is pale golden. Leave to cool.

**3** To make the crème patissière, use a small sharp knife to scrape the seeds from the vanilla pod. Cook the vanilla pod, seeds and milk in a small saucepan set over a medium heat, stirring, for 5 minutes or until the mixture just comes to a simmer. Take the pan off the heat, cover with the lid and set aside for 20 minutes to infuse, then remove the vanilla pod.

**4** Combine the egg yolk, flour and sugar in a bowl and whisk with a hand-held electric whisk until thick and pale. Next, whisk in the infused milk. Heat the mixture in a clean saucepan set over a medium heat. Cook, stirring continuously, for 4–5 minutes or until the mixture boils and thickens, then strain it through a fine sieve into a bowl and cover the surface with clingfilm to prevent a skin from forming. Chill in the refrigerator for 40 minutes.

**5** Remove the cream from the refrigerator and whisk it until it is smooth. Add the thick cream and continue to whisk until it is well combined. Spoon the crème patissière evenly between the 24 pastry cases. Top each tart with a raspberry and dust with icing sugar, if desired. Serve immediately.

# Maraschino Cookies

MAKES 18
PREP 20 mins, plus chilling
COOK 15 mins

115g (4oz) butter, softened

100g (3½oz) caster sugar

50g (1¾oz) dark muscovado sugar

¼ tsp salt

1 free-range egg

1 tsp vanilla extract

150g (5½oz) plain flour

55g (2oz) cocoa powder

¼ tsp bicarbonate of soda

¼ tsp baking powder

18 maraschino or glacé cherries

**1** Preheat the oven to 200°C/fan 180°C/gas mark 6. Line 2 baking sheets with nonstick baking paper.

**2** Cream the butter and sugars together with a wooden spoon or an electric whisk until light and fluffy. Add the salt, egg and vanilla extract and beat well.

**3** In a separate bowl, combine the flour, cocoa powder, bicarbonate of soda and baking powder. Slowly fold the dry ingredients into the creamed butter mixture until a smooth dough forms. It should be solid enough to hold its shape when rolled into a ball. Wrap the dough in clingfilm and chill in the refrigerator for 30 minutes.

**4** Remove the dough from the refrigerator, unwrap it and roll it into 18 balls that are roughly 3cm (1¼in) in diameter. Place these on the prepared baking sheet. Using your thumb, make a small cherry-sized indentation in the top of each ball of dough. Place a cherry in each of these indentations.

**5** Bake the cookies for 15 minutes. Take them out of the oven and leave them to cool for about 5 minutes, then transfer the cookies to a wire rack to cool completely.

# Red Velvet Layer Cake

50g (1¾oz) unsalted butter, softened, plus extra for greasing

125g (4½oz) caster sugar

1 free-range egg, beaten

1 tsp vanilla extract

75g (2¾oz) plain flour, plus extra for dusting

1½ tbsp cocoa powder

1 tsp bicarbonate of soda

pinch of salt

2 tsp red food colouring

60ml (2¼fl oz) buttermilk

**For the icing**

50g (1¾oz) unsalted butter, softened

100g (3½oz) cream cheese

200g (7oz) icing sugar

½ tsp vanilla extract

50g (1¾oz) pecans, chopped

MAKES 6
PREP 15 mins
COOK 30 mins

**1** Preheat the oven to 180°C/fan 160ºC/gas mark 4. Grease and flour a 20cm (8in) square loose-bottomed cake tin. Cream the butter and sugar together with a wooden spoon or an electric whisk until light and fluffy. Beat in the egg and vanilla extract. Sift the flour, cocoa, bicarbonate of soda and salt into a separate bowl. Stir the colouring into the buttermilk, then mix this and the flour mixture alternately into the creamed mixture. Pour the batter into the tin and bake for 25–30 minutes until firm. Allow the cake to cool in the tin for 10 minutes, then turn it out on a wire rack and let it cool completely.

**2** For the icing, beat the butter and cream cheese together in a bowl. Beat in the icing sugar and vanilla extract.

**3** Halve the sponge into 2 × 10cm- (4in-) wide pieces. Cut each half into 5 × 4cm- (1½in-) wide rectangles, to give you 10 4cm × 10cm (1½in × 4in) rectangles. Halve each piece horizontally – you now have 20 rectangles, each measuring 4cm × 10cm (1½in × 4in). Build up each mini layer cake using 3 rectangles of cake (you'll have 2 pieces left over) and sandwich each layer with the icing. Ice the top, sprinkle with the chopped pecans and serve.

Maraschino Cookies

Raspberry Custard Tarts

Dreaming

H Scott

WORDS BY
ANTHONY STEPHAN
MUSIC BY
MIGUEL,

Red Velvet Layer Cakes

The moments spent sharing cocktails and laughing with your girlfriends will live on in your heart forever. On this incredibly special occasion, these cocktails really do take to the stage and sing out to be tasted. Be creative with your friends' favourite drinks and flavours. My favourite drink is Champagne, and adding a heart-shaped ice cube of any flavour really makes it special! For those with the bonbon bug, my Devil Drinks Martini cocktail is delicious. And why not take it one note higher with the Chocolate-covered Cherry Martini?

# THE DEVIL DRINKS MARTINI

5 ice cubes
30ml (1fl oz) black vodka
30ml (1fl oz) cherry juice
raspberries and blueberries,
to decorate

**1** Combine the ice cubes, vodka and cherry juice in a cocktail shaker; shake for 5–10 seconds.

**2** Pour the mixture into a martini glass.

**3** Thread raspberries and blueberries onto a cocktail stick and place them in the drink. Serve immediately.

# CHOCOLATE-covered CHERRY MARTINI

FOR ALL THREE COCKTAILS:

MAKES 1

PREP 5 mins

1 tbsp chocolate syrup

3 maraschino cherries

30ml (1fl oz) chocolate vodka
(use regular vodka if you can't find this)

30ml (1fl oz) cherry vodka

30ml (1fl oz) crème de cacao

1 tbsp double cream

5 ice cubes

**1** Swirl the chocolate syrup around inside a martini glass and place the cherries in the bottom of the glass.

**2** Pour all the liquids with the ice into a cocktail shaker and shake for 5–10 seconds.

**3** Pour the drink into the prepared martini glass. Serve immediately.

# HEARTS & CHAMPAGNE

PREP add **3** hours' freezing time for the ice cubes

150–200ml (¼–⅓ pint) strawberry juice or other red-coloured juice

1 × 750ml bottle of Champagne, chilled

**1** A few hours before the party, fill an ice-cube tray with heart-shaped moulds with your chosen juice and place it in the freezer until completely frozen.

**2** Drop a few frozen hearts into 6 Champagne flutes and top up with Champagne. Serve immediately.

Hearts & Champagne

Chocolate-covered
Cherry Martini

If you can imagine drinking a delicious iced vodka with your favourite red juice while watching a ruby sunset on a black night, then you can imagine exactly what this drink has in store for you!

# CRANBERRY & VODKA THE HEN PARTY WAY

SERVES **1** | PREP **2** mins

5 ice cubes

125ml (4fl oz) cranberry juice

50ml (2fl oz) black vodka

**1** Place the ice in a tumbler and pour the cranberry juice over the top.

**2** Pour the vodka over the back of a teaspoon into the glass so that it sits on top of the juice and creates a layer of black. Serve immediately.

# How to Make a Mini Top Hat

I often find myself in a haberdashery being wooed by the exciting products. Lately, they've started selling hats. I can't help but look, touch and enquire how much (always gulping when I'm told). Our cute top hats are easy to make and, when styled with a fabulous hair-do, are perfect for a night of frivolity.

## YOU WILL NEED

✂ pencil ✂ 2 plates – 1 the size you would like the brim of your top hat to be, the other about 5cm (2in) smaller ✂ 3 sheets of black A4 card ✂ craft knife ✂ cutting mat ✂ glue gun ✂ metal ruler ✂ paper scissors ✂ 50cm (½yd) black felt or black felted paper ✂ fabric scissors ✂ ribbons, lace, feathers or flowers (optional) ✂ comb hair slide ✂ short piece of thin elastic ✂ needle ✂ hair clip

**1** Draw a circle around the larger plate onto the black card and cut it out. Draw another circle around the small plate inside the circle you've already drawn. Cut out the inner circle using a craft knife and cutting mat, creating a doughnut-shaped piece (piece A).

**2** Using more black card, form a cylinder. The mouth of the cylinder should be as big as the inner circle in piece A. Glue the 2 long edges of the cylinder together. The height of the cylinder depends on how tall you would like the top hat to be. This makes piece B.

**3** Cut 3cm- (1¼in-) long vertical slits around 1 end of the cylinder, spacing them 1cm (½in) apart, to form flaps.

**4** Push cylindrical piece B through doughnut-shaped piece A. Bend back the flaps on piece B and secure them to piece A with glue.

**5** To make the top of the hat, use the open part of the hat as a template. Draw around it onto the remaining card. Draw a larger circle around this one (use the large plate as a template). Cut out the larger circle.

**6** Cut short vertical slits, each around 2cm (¾in) long, from the rim inwards towards the inner circle, to create flaps. Use this piece (piece C) to cover the hole in the top of the hat, folding over the flaps and gluing them down inside the hat.

**7** You can now cover your hat with felt to give it a clean finish and hide all the folded seams. Cut shapes out from the felt, or felted paper, as before, omitting the flaps, and stick these onto the cardboard hat with a glue gun. At this point you may wish to add other decorative details, such as ribbons, lace, feathers or flowers, to give your top hat a feminine touch.

**8** Glue a comb hair slide on 1 side of the underside of the hat so that it can be pushed into the hair.

**9** Thread the elastic through the needle. Attach an elastic loop that's no more than 5mm (¼in) long to the hat on the opposite side to the hair slide by sewing a single stitch onto the hat and tying a knot. Push a hair clip through this to secure the hat in place.

# How to Make a
# MOTHER-of-PEARL LAMPSHADE

On my quest to adopt Britain's lost treasures, I often find beautiful lamp bases with tired old shades, desperate for a style make-over. This shade's new look comes from mother-of-pearl shells, which give it a truly magical glow. I spent months searching the coast for the shells. Actually, that's a lie! You can buy a variety of shells by weight online, so pick them to complement your base.

## YOU WILL NEED

✂ working lamp ✂ florist's cellophane ✂ sharp scissors ✂ glue gun

✂ mother-of-pearl shells (the quantity will depend on the size of your shade)

✂ fire-retardant spray ✂ low-wattage light bulb (25 watts or less)

1 Remove the current cover from your lampshade, stripping it back to the wire frame.

2 Cover all the panels on the frame with cellophane, creating an invisible base for your shells to sit on. To do this, cut a piece of cellophane that is roughly 5cm (2in) larger than the panel. Apply glue around the wire edge where you will need to attach the cellophane. Lay the cellophane over the panel, carefully pressing it down from the top to the bottom to ensure it is flat. Use the scissors to cut off the excess cellophane to produce a neat finish that fits the frame perfectly. Repeat this step on all the panels until your lampshade is entirely covered with cellophane.

3 To cover the lampshade with the shells, put a small blob of glue on the back of each shell and position it on the cellophane. Working around your shade, start from the bottom and decorate the full circumference of the base with 1 row of shells, then work your way up the lampshade. Try to use similar-sized shells in each row to produce an even finish. Overlap each shell slightly to minimize the number of gaps.

4 When the lampshade is totally covered, carefully check for any obvious gaps and use smaller shells to fill them in. Allow the glue to dry thoroughly, then spray the entire lampshade with a coat of fire-retardant spray.

5 Now you're finished and ready to put your beautiful lampshade back on the lamp base.

**NOTE** Make sure you use only low-wattage light bulbs (25 watts or less) with this lamp.

# HOW TO CREATE
# THE CARMEN MIRANDA

Look to the tantalizing world of cabaret for inspiration for your hen party hair-dos. Taking inspiration from the golden age of show girls, with their sparkling costumes and elaborate headpieces and hats, will transform your hen party into a decadent farewell to the bride-to-be's fabulous single days. Carmen Miranda was the poster girl for camp, being flamboyant and an embodiment of the true spirit of carnival! Her outlandish costumes and headpieces wowed American war-time audiences. Use her as your muse for your party preparations and be as creative as you dare.

## YOU WILL NEED

✎ hair mousse ✎ tail comb ✎ curling tongs ✎ hair grips and hairpins ✎ hat of your choice
✎ bristle brush ✎ hairband ✎ section clips ✎ hairspray

△ **STEP 1** Curl and set your hair (*see* page 100) to give it a wave. Separate the front central section by making 2 partings above your eyebrows to meet at the crown. Divide the section across the top of the head into 2 large pin curls (they don't have to be neat, as they are a base for the hat) and secure the curls with hair grips.

△ **STEP 2** Position the hat and, if needed, use hair grips to secure it.

▽ **STEP 3** Make a diagonal parting from where the crown meets the back of the hat to the front of your ear.

△ **STEP 4** Backcomb this and smooth the surface with a bristle brush.

△ **STEP 5** Roll this section of hair forwards to form a curl at the base of the hat, using your thumb to shape the loop. Pin this curl into place.

△ **STEP 6** Make another diagonal parting 5cm (2in) parallel to the first and repeat steps 4 and 5. Repeat steps 3, 4, 5 and 6 on the other side of your head.

△ **STEP 7** Part the remaining hair horizontally 5cm (2in) below the bottom of the hat. Secure the top section with a hairband and clip it out of the way for now.

△ **STEP 8** Sweep the remaining hair upwards to meet the ponytail and pin it into place with a horizontal line of hair grips, smoothing the hair with a brush and spraying any flyaway strands into place with hairspray. Divide this section into 3 and roll each into flat curls at the back of the head, pinning them into place. Leaving the ponytail until last, bring this curl up to meet the base of the hat and pin it into place.

WEDDING TEA PARTY

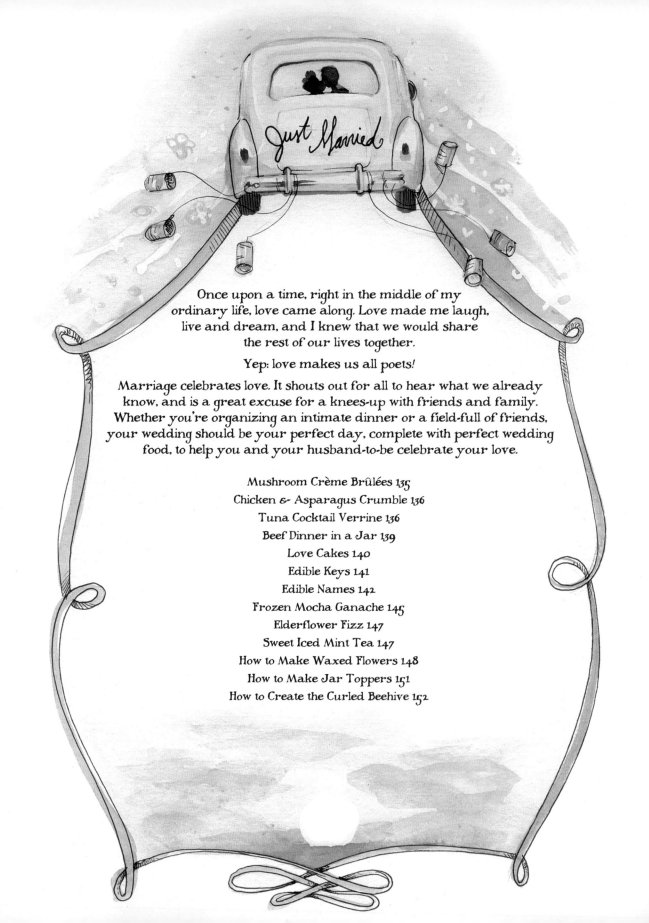

Once upon a time, right in the middle of my
ordinary life, love came along. Love made me laugh,
live and dream, and I knew that we would share
the rest of our lives together.

*Yep: love makes us all poets!*

Marriage celebrates love. It shouts out for all to hear what we already
know, and is a great excuse for a knees-up with friends and family.
Whether you're organizing an intimate dinner or a field-full of friends,
your wedding should be your perfect day, complete with perfect wedding
food, to help you and your husband-to-be celebrate your love.

PUT YOUR
PHOTO HERE

The taste of savoury custard and a sweet caramel crunch is surprisingly fabulous. Your taste-bud journey begins with sweet, sharp sherry vinegar and finishes with the creamy woodiness of mushrooms. Cooking this dish in old condiment pots is visually enchanting – a great way to begin your wedding meal.

# MUSHROOM CRÈME BRÛLÉES

**MAKES** 6

**PREP** 20 mins, plus soaking

**COOK** 1 hour

good handful of dried mushrooms, such as cep or porcini

275ml (9½fl oz) milk

150ml (¼ pint) double cream

4 free-range egg yolks

salt and black pepper

pinch of ground nutmeg

3 tbsp demerara sugar

**For the garnish**

100ml (3½fl oz) sherry vinegar

4 tbsp caster sugar

handful of exotic mushrooms

**1** Put the dried mushrooms into a bowl. Heat 150ml (¼ pint) of the milk in a small saucepan until it is just boiling, then pour it over the mushrooms. Soak them for at least 1½–2 hours. Keep pushing the mushrooms down under the milk's surface to ensure they all soften.

**2** Once the milk has been absorbed, process the mushrooms into a paste in a food processor, then pass this through a sieve. Set aside.

**3** Preheat the oven to 120°C/ fan 100°C/gas mark ½. Heat the remaining milk with the cream on the hob to a gentle boil. Take the pan off the heat, add the mushroom paste and whisk until the ingredients are well combined.

**4** In a separate bowl, whisk the egg yolks. Continue to whisk as you slowly pour in the mushroom mixture. Season and add the nutmeg.

**5** Pour the mixture into 6 decorative jars, dishes or small teacups. Place these in a roasting tin and pour hot water into the tin until the water reaches approximately halfway up the outsides of the containers.

**6** Bake for 1 hour or until set (the custard has set if there is a gentle wobble when it is shaken). Allow the custard to cool slightly, then sprinkle over the demerara sugar. Charge up the kitchen blow torch and caramelize the sugar.

**7** Meanwhile, for the garnish, heat the vinegar and sugar in a saucepan until reduced to a syrupy sauce. Add the mushrooms and cook for a further 3–4 minutes. Place on top of the brûlées.

Serving creamy crumble is a wise move on your wedding day – it solves any "dry chicken" problems and will soak up the wedding fizz!

# CHICKEN & ASPARAGUS CRUMBLE

**SERVES** 6

**PREP** 15 mins

**COOK** 20 mins

50g (1¾oz) butter

600g (1lb 5oz) chicken breast, cut into 2cm (¾in) cubes

50g (1¾oz) plain flour

400ml (14fl oz) whole milk

200g (7oz) asparagus spears, trimmed and cut into 2cm (¾in) lengths

grated rind of ½ lemon

2 tbsp chopped tarragon

salt and black pepper

**For the crumble**

100g (3½oz) butter, chilled and cubed

200g (7oz) wholemeal flour, seasoned with salt and black pepper

**1** Preheat the oven to 180°C/fan 160°C/gas mark 4. For the crumble, rub the butter into the seasoned flour until clumps form and most of the butter is rubbed in. Spread across a baking tray and cook for 15–20 minutes, stirring halfway through the cooking time to form big lumps.

**2** Meanwhile, melt the butter in a pan and add the chicken cubes. Stir and cook for 4 minutes. Sprinkle the flour over the chicken and cook, stirring, for 3 more minutes. Take the pan off the heat and slowly stir in the milk.

**3** Return the pan to the heat and bring to the boil, stirring, then add the asparagus, lemon rind and tarragon and cook for 3–5 minutes until the sauce thickens to the consistency of lightly whipped double cream. Season to taste.

**4** Divide the chicken between 6 plates. Top with the crumble mixture and serve.

Over the years I've attended many weddings, and prawn cocktail appears never to go out of wedding fashion – it's such a crowd-pleaser. I was desperate to find a delicious alternative, and I must thank my good friend Chris for sharing her Asian-inspired tuna cocktail. The flavours and textures of this dish (which is easy to prepare and serve en masse) take you out of this world or, at least, out of this country.

# TUNA COCKTAIL VERRINE

**SERVES** 6

**PREP** 15 mins, plus chilling

300g (10½oz) good-quality raw tuna, cut into 1cm (½in) cubes

juice and grated rind of 3 limes, plus extra grated lime rind to garnish

3 tbsp sesame seeds, lightly toasted

1 red chilli, thinly sliced

3 tbsp roughly chopped fresh coriander

1 tbsp sesame oil

3 avocados, peeled, stoned and diced

200ml (⅓ pint) coconut cream

**1** Add the tuna to the lime juice and rind in a large non-reactive bowl and toss them together. Add the sesame seeds, chilli, coriander and sesame oil and toss the mixture again.

**2** Add the avocados and mix them together gently with the other ingredients. Add the coconut cream.

**3** Chill the mixture for at least an hour, then put into serving glasses, garnish with a little extra grated lime rind and serve.

Imagine the scene: it's your big day, the day you may have dreamed about since you were a child; you are surrounded by the people you love; everything is so beautiful and elegant, drowning you in a sea of glamour... What's on the menu? Beef in a Jar, of course! This dish may not be for everyone, but it's tasty and, for me, it represents the bad sense of humour I inherited from my father. Your personality should be part of your big day, so you decide what food you'd like to share with your guests. The best wedding I ever attended served fish and chips in newspaper; can't get better than that, right?!

# Beef Dinner in a Jar

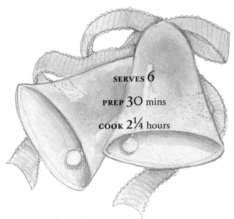

**SERVES** 6

**PREP** 30 mins

**COOK** 2¼ hours

3 tbsp olive oil

600g (1lb 5oz) beef shin, cut into 2cm (¾in) cubes

1 onion, roughly diced

50g (1¾oz) plain flour

about 500ml (18fl oz) red wine

3 tbsp tomato purée

3 sprigs of rosemary

500g (1lb 2oz) potatoes, peeled and cut into chunks

salt

100g (3½oz) butter

3 tbsp horseradish sauce

150g (5½oz) French beans, trimmed and halved

**1** Heat 2 tablespoons of the oil in a large flameproof casserole until hot, then add the beef in batches and brown for 5 minutes. Remove from the casserole with a slotted spoon and set aside. Cook the onion in the remaining oil for 5–7 minutes until softened.

**2** Sprinkle the flour over the onion and cook, stirring, for a further 3 minutes. Slowly pour in the red wine while stirring.

**3** Return the beef to the casserole with the tomato purée and rosemary. Stir, cover and simmer for about 2 hours. Occasionally check to stir and ensure the liquid has not all evaporated; add a little more wine if necessary. Add salt to taste.

**4** Meanwhile, boil the potatoes in salted water until tender but not falling apart. Drain and finely mash them with the butter and horseradish sauce. Use a piping bag to pipe the mash into 6 decorative jars, ensuring it's up against the side all the way around the jar.

**5** Blanch the beans for 2 minutes in a pan of salted water. Top the mash in the jars with the beef and, finally, the beans, then serve.

# Love cakes

MAKES **16**

PREP **20** mins

COOK **50** mins

We recently hosted a Sri Lankan wedding in London.
It was The Vintage Patisserie at its best. Our wedding favours were pretty
boxes of traditional Sri Lankan love cake, to symbolize fertility, longevity, wealth, health
and happiness. I was uplifted by this fragrant cake and have adopted it into my family.

125g (4½oz) butter, softened,
plus extra for greasing

3 free-range eggs, separated

150g (5½oz) caster sugar

125g (4½oz) semolina

50g (1¾oz) cashews, crushed

1 tbsp rosewater

1 tbsp honey

1½ tbsp brandy

½ tsp ground cinnamon

½ tsp ground cardamom

½ tsp ground nutmeg

icing sugar, for dusting

**1** Preheat the oven to 150°C/fan 130°C/gas mark 2. Grease a 20cm (8in) square cake tin and line the base with nonstick baking paper.

**2** Beat together the softened butter, the egg yolks and caster sugar. Add the semolina, cashew nuts, rosewater, honey, brandy and spices.

**3** In a grease-free bowl, whisk the egg whites until stiff peaks form.

**4** Stir a large spoonful of the egg whites into the cake mixture, then fold in the rest, trying to keep as much air in the mixture as possible. Pour the batter into the prepared tin and bake for 50 minutes until it is golden and firm to the touch and starting to come away from the sides of the tin.

**5** Turn off the oven and leave the door ajar to allow the cake to cool down slowly.

**6** Once cool, invert the cake tin onto a chopping board and cut the cake into 16 squares. Dust these with icing sugar before popping each into a favour box.

MAKES
100

PREP
2–3
mins
per key

Rusty old keys excite me.
I wish they could talk so that
I could discover their stories
and secrets. Keys, which unlock
new journeys in our lives, are
so appropriate at a wedding. Use
a silicone key mould (available
online) and follow this recipe
to create your own.

# EDIbLe Keys

500g (1lb 2oz) marzipan
edible gold lustre spray (available online)

**1** Break a small piece of marzipan off the block and press it into a silicone key mould. Using a chocolate scraper, gently scrape the excess marzipan off the mould to give you a flat surface.

**2** Pull the silicone back at the top of the key so that the marzipan pops out. Gently ease it out of the mould

and transfer it to a tray lined with nonstick baking paper. Straighten the key if necessary. Repeat with the remaining marzipan.

**3** Leave the keys to harden overnight, then spray them with edible gold lustre.

I can't take the credit for this genius idea, but I'm totally in love with it! There will be certain grand impressions from the big event captured in the mind's eye of your guests forever, and a Scrabble board, complete with delicious biscuit tiles spelling out heartfelt messages of love, will be one of them. I like to keep the biscuit base simple and classic to show off its personality.

# Edible Names

450g (1lb) plain flour, plus extra for dusting

½ tsp baking powder

pinch of salt

225g (8oz) vanilla sugar

225g (8oz) salted butter, softened

1 free-range egg

¾ tsp vanilla extract

½ tsp almond extract

**For the icing**

2 free-range egg whites

450g (1lb) icing sugar, sifted

2 tsp lemon juice

1 tsp glycerine

ready-made black piping icing or black icing pens

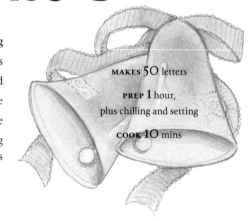

MAKES 50 letters

PREP 1 hour, plus chilling and setting

COOK 10 mins

**1** Preheat the oven to 180°C/fan 160°C/gas mark 4.

**2** Mix together the flour, baking powder and salt in a large bowl. Set the mixture aside.

**3** Cream the butter and sugar together with a wooden spoon or an electric whisk until light and fluffy. Beat in the egg and the vanilla and almond extracts. Gradually fold in the flour mixture to form a crumbly dough.

**4** Knead the dough, roll it into a ball, wrap it in clingfilm and place it in the refrigerator to chill for 30 minutes.

**5** Roll out the dough on a lightly floured surface and cut it into 50 squares, each the size of a Scrabble tile. Place these on baking sheets lined with nonstick baking paper and put them in the freezer for 15 minutes to set.

**6** Bake the Scrabble tiles for 8–10 minutes until golden. Allow them to cool for a few minutes on the baking sheets, then transfer them to a wire rack.

**7** To make the icing, whisk the egg whites in a large bowl until they become frothy. Beat in the icing sugar a spoonful at a time. Add the lemon juice and glycerine and keep beating until the mixture becomes very stiff and the whites stand up in peaks.

**8** If necessary, thin the icing by stirring in a teaspoon of water at a time until it becomes a good consistency for icing the biscuits. Cover the icing with a damp tea towel and let it sit for several minutes. Using a small teaspoon, place a dollop of icing in the centre of a biscuit, then gently spread it out across the surface, working out towards the edges, with a cocktail stick. Repeat for the rest of the biscuits. Allow the icing to set for at least 1 hour.

**9** Pipe the letters to spell out the words you will be making onto the squares using black icing and an even thinner nozzle, or icing pens. Add the point value for each letter in the corner of the tile for authenticity.

A good wedding meal with speeches can go on for hours and, often, by tea and coffee time (and with plenty of booze under the belt), the guests have left their seats behind and are having a party. Serving Frozen Mocha Ganache is a delicious way to tempt them back to their seats. If you want to offer a choice of flavours, think Green Jasmine.

# Frozen Mocha Ganache

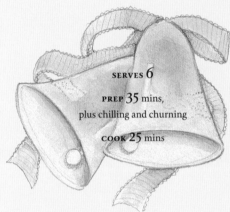

SERVES 6

PREP 35 mins,
plus chilling and churning

COOK 25 mins

250g (9oz) dark chocolate,
roughly chopped

75ml (2½fl oz) very strong hot
coffee (3 double espressos or 6 tsp
instant coffee mixed with 75ml/
2½fl oz hot water)

500ml (18fl oz) single cream

250ml (9fl oz) double cream

150g (5½oz) caster sugar

4 free-range egg yolks

### For the ganache

100ml (3½fl oz) single cream

50g (1¾oz) dark chocolate,
finely chopped

100ml (3½fl oz) double cream

1 Break the chocolate into pieces and melt it in a heatproof bowl set over a saucepan of barely simmering water, ensuring the base of the bowl doesn't touch the water below. Stir in the coffee and set aside.

2 Slowly bring the creams and 100g (3½oz) of the sugar to the boil in a heavy-based saucepan set over a low heat, stirring until the sugar dissolves.

3 In a bowl, beat the egg yolks and remaining sugar with a hand-held electric whisk set on a high speed until the mixture is thick and pale. Reduce the speed and gradually pour in the hot cream mixture, whisking continuously.

4 Return this custard to the saucepan and cook over a medium heat, stirring continuously, for 6–8 minutes until the mixture thickens and coats the back of a wooden spoon.

5 Remove the custard from heat and stir it into the chocolate–coffee mixture. Immediately cover the mixture with clingfilm, ensuring it is flush with the custard's surface to prevent a skin from forming. Allow to cool, then chill in the refrigerator for 3 hours. Transfer to an ice-cream maker and follow the manufacturer's instructions to churn it.

6 Scoop the ice cream into 6 coffee cups and smooth out the surface. Store the cups in the freezer.

7 To make the ganache, heat the cream and chocolate in a small saucepan set over a low heat. Stir continuously until the chocolate has melted, then allow the mixture to cool.

8 Pour a thin layer of ganache over the ice cream. Put a drop of cream on top, swirl it into a design, then replace the cups in the freezer until 15 minutes prior to serving.

Elderflowers are as happy growing on roadsides as they are in gardens so, wherever you are, you can enjoy making your own fizz! Fresh flowers are restricted to summertime, so use dried flowers, if necessary, doubling the quantity. The finished product is musky, yet fruity and easy to drink in copious amounts. For something lighter but equally refreshing, try my Sweet Iced Mint Tea, and for a winter wedding, add hot water instead!

# ELDERFLOWER FIZZ

**MAKES 6** bottles
of varying sizes

**PREP 15** mins,
plus soaking and maturing

600ml (1 pint) compressed
elderflowers

675g (1lb 8oz) granulated
sugar

zested rind and juice of
2 lemons

2 tbsp white wine vinegar

**EQUIPMENT**

large container that holds
4.5 litres (8 pints)

zester

jug

sieve

funnel

plastic pop bottles, sterilized

**1** Mix the elderflowers with 4.5 litres (8 pints) water and stir thoroughly. Add the sugar and stir it until most of it has dissolved. Add the lemon rind and juice and the vinegar. Cover the container and leave it in a warm place for 24 hours.

**2** Strain the liquid and pour it into sterilized bottles.

**3** Leave the bottles for 2 weeks, checking them daily to ensure the bottles are not too full. If they are, gently release some of the gas. Consume the drink within 1 month.

# SWEET ICED MINT TEA

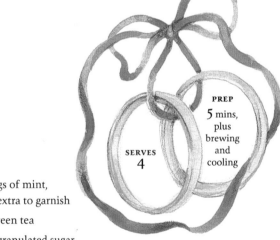

**SERVES 4**

**PREP 5** mins, plus brewing and cooling

10 sprigs of mint,
plus 4 extra to garnish

3 tsp green tea

3 tbsp granulated sugar

**1** Boil 1 litre (1¾ pints) water. Pour a small amount into a teapot and swish it around to warm the pot, then discard.

**2** Combine the mint, green tea and sugar in the teapot, then fill it with the rest of the hot water. Let the tea brew, stirring the leaves once or twice, for 3 minutes.

**3** Pour the tea through a tea strainer into teacups and allow to cool. Garnish with the remaining mint sprigs.

# How to Make Waxed Flowers

You can capture a fresh flower's beauty and make it last by using a simple waxing technique, and your guest can take home a floral tribute to the day. Some of the best flowers to use are roses, daisies, thistles, tulips, hyacinths, stephanotis and other flowers that have a natural waxy coating. Leaves and hardy plants always wax well, so don't be afraid to try out a selection – just avoid very delicate flowers that will wither in the heat of the wax.

## YOU WILL NEED

bowl ✿ paraffin wax ✿ saucepan ✿ disposable wooden stick or skewer for stirring the wax ✿ thermometer ✿ nonstick baking paper ✿ selection of fresh, firm flowers and leaf clusters ✿ scissors ✿ jar filled with water ✿ bowl of iced water ✿ container in which to arrange the display

1 Fill a glass bowl three-quarters full with paraffin wax and set it over a saucepan of barely simmering water, ensuring the base of the bowl doesn't touch the water below. Use a wooden stick or skewer to stir the paraffin until it becomes liquid. Put your thermometer into the wax and leave it there – you need to get it to 54–60°C (130–140°F) and maintain it.

2 Lay out a sheet of nonstick baking paper over an area of your work surface.

3 Clip the flower stems 13cm (5in) below the calyx and set them in a jar of water. Clip and set aside a selection of attractive leaf clusters.

4 Hold a flower upside down by its stem and dip it into the warm wax without touching the flower to the side of the bowl. Hold the flower in the wax for 2–3 seconds. Remove the flower, gently shake off any excess wax, then dip it into a bowl of iced water and lift out. Place your flower on its side on the baking paper for about 5 minutes to harden completely. Once the wax has hardened, gently hold the flower head and dip the stem in and out of the wax to coat the entire flower. Repeat the same process with all the flowers and leaves. If you're waxing a flower that has many petals, spoon wax into the centre of the flower after dipping to ensure full coverage.

5 Once you're happy with your flowers, they can be used to create a beautiful and lasting display.

# How to make Jar Toppers

Jars are one of the things I like to collect that actually have a use. I've often covered jar lids in fabric and added a pretty label to give homemade jams and other stuff as gifts. A few years ago, when I rediscovered my glue gun, I went a bit crazy and glued everything to everything! And jars – you don't get away! Whatever your occasion, this is a fantastic way of adding the personal touch to a jar of something delicious.

### YOU WILL NEED

≫ selection of empty glass food jars with screw-on lids ≫ selection of themed jar toppers ≫ glue gun ≫ newspaper or scrap paper ≫ spray paints in celebratory colours, such as red, gold, green and silver

**1** Collect some empty food jars with screw-on lids – a selection of varying shapes and sizes makes an attractive display. When you are happy with your jars, ensure they are washed thoroughly.

**2** Find some items to use as jar toppers – old Christmas decorations or collected pine cones work well. For weddings, you can find themed toppers in cake shops.

**3** Next, use a glue gun to glue 1 topper to each of your jar lids and allow them to dry thoroughly.

**4** Unscrew and remove the embellished lids from your jars, sit the lids on some newspaper or scrap paper in a well-ventilated area and spray the lids and their toppers with the spray paints. Spray a little at a time, coming back to add more coats if necessary (this avoids any unwanted clumps of paint).

**5** When the lids and their toppers are dry and you are happy with the finish, simply fill the jars with treats, drinks, dinners… anything you like!

# HOW TO CREATE THE
## CURLED BEEHIVE

Just as important as your dress is your wedding-day hair and make-up. With so much choice for vintage hair inspiration, whether you are using a hair stylist or doing it yourself, it's really worth investing time in finding your perfect hairstyle for the big day. Our advice is to stick to your preferred style decade and just go for it! Our model for this look is a true 60s belle, so embracing that, along with the timeless chic of the era, we present "The Curled Beehive".

### YOU WILL NEED

hair mousse ✎ tail comb ✎ heated rollers ✎ section clips ✎ hair rat, if your hair is too fine to create a structured beehive (available in pharmacies and online) ✎ bristle brush ✎ hairpins and grips ✎ hairspray ✎ decorative hair slides, flowers or jewels

◁ **STEP 1** Curl and set your hair with heated rollers for a loose wave (*see* page 100). Ensure the rollers at the centre-front of the head are rolled backwards to create as much volume as possible. If you have a fringe, style it at this stage.

▷ **STEP 2** Remove the rollers and section the hair from ear to ear across the head. Divide the front section into 3 with 2 partings above each brow. Ensure each section is evenly sized.

◁ **STEP 3** If using a hair rat, attach it now. Take a handful of hair from one side of the head, just behind the parting, backcomb and smooth it, then sweep it to the opposite side of the head (over the hair rat, if using). Secure with pins in a vertical line down the middle of the head.

▷ **STEP 4**
Repeat step 3 on the other side and pin to create the base of the beehive. Spray with hairspray to secure.

◁ **STEP 5**
Working on the front sections one at a time, repeat steps 3 and 4, backcombing the hair from behind and smoothing the strands backwards with a bristle brush, to pin the hair securely over the beehive.

▷ **STEP 6** Using the hair at the back of the head, loop sections up to create pin curls that meet the beehive. Secure with hairpins. We have left some hair loose for a soft, feminine look, but this style works just as well with all the hair pinned up off the neck. Decorate the beehive with chic hair slides, flowers or jewels.

Nature's most romantic gift is certainly a baby.
Life takes on new meaning and direction on the birth
of a child. Friends and family await the announcement of
the birth with anticipation, eager to bear love and gifts. Everyone
wants to care for mum-to-be and show her how special she is to be bringing a
new person into the world. Baby showers have become increasingly popular
in the UK, especially over the last five years. We have borrowed the occasion
from our friends over the pond, who celebrate a pregnancy and impending
birth with this event, in which the mum-to-be, at centre stage, is showered
with gifts from her friends for the soon-to-be-born baby. My uber-glamorous
take on the occasion celebrates the very special mum-to-be in style, and
surrounds her with loved ones, delicious food and lots of laughter.

thank you

Tarte Tatin excites me on many levels. Firstly, the variety of flavours you can play with is endless – I love this savoury version with sweet roasted peppers, courgette and a kick of Parmesan; it's truly heavenly! Secondly, I love the suspense of not seeing the finished product until the end. Allow yourself time to arrange the vegetables in pretty spirals – do this early in the day and add the pastry when your guests arrive, so you have more time to relax.

# MINI SAVOURY TARTE TATIN

**SERVES** 6 (2 tarts each)

**PREP** 20 mins,
plus cooling and salting

**COOK** 1 hour

1 red pepper
1 yellow pepper
1 tbsp olive oil
black pepper
1 small courgette
150g (5½oz) mozzarella cheese, roughly torn
1 tbsp grated Parmesan cheese
plain flour, for dusting
375g (13oz) shop-bought all-butter puff pastry

**1** Preheat the oven to 190°C/fan 170°C/gas mark 5.

**2** Place the peppers on a baking tray, drizzle them with the oil, sprinkle over some salt and roast them for about 45 minutes until the skins are nearly black. Remove the peppers from the oven, place them in a plastic food bag, seal the bag and set it aside for about 30 minutes to cool (this makes it easier to remove the skins). When they have cooled down, peel the peppers and cut them into strips about 1cm (½in) wide.

**3** Using a vegetable peeler, slice the courgette lengthways into ribbons that are just thin enough to roll up. If the slices are too thin to roll properly, use a knife to slice the courgette to the right thickness. Place the courgette slices on a plate, sprinkle them with salt and set aside for 20 minutes. Then wash the courgette under cold running water and dry on kitchen paper.

**4** Roll a strip of pepper inside a strip of courgette, trimming the strips to the same width, and pop 2 rolls in each of the cups of a 12-cup Yorkshire pudding tin (its cups should be roughly 6cm (2½in) in diameter). Scatter over the mozzarella and Parmesan cheeses.

**5** Roll out the pastry on a floured work surface to a thickness of about 5mm (¼in). Using a round pastry cutter that's about 1cm (½in) wider than the cups of your tin, stamp out 12 discs. Gently press 1 disc over each cup. Bake for 15–20 minutes until the pastry is puffed up and golden. Serve with a grinding of black pepper.

Apart from my nan's chicken soup, pea and ham is top of the comfort-soup chart for me – and it's incredibly simple to make! Personally, I don't think about seasoning until the end, as the ham hock itself is salty, so the dish often needs no extra salt. Serve this soup with homemade Scone Rarebit (*see* opposite) in simple teacups, and you can't help but make people happy.

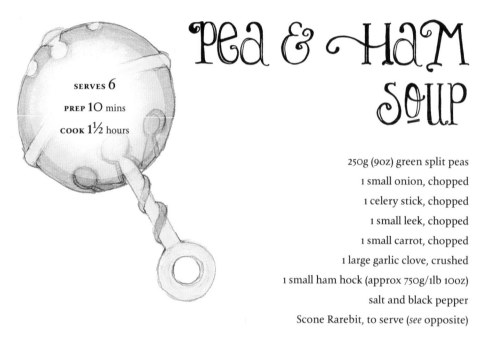

# Pea & Ham Soup

**SERVES** 6

**PREP** 10 mins

**COOK** 1½ hours

250g (9oz) green split peas

1 small onion, chopped

1 celery stick, chopped

1 small leek, chopped

1 small carrot, chopped

1 large garlic clove, crushed

1 small ham hock (approx 750g/1lb 10oz)

salt and black pepper

Scone Rarebit, to serve (*see* opposite)

**1** Place all the ingredients except the seasoning in a large saucepan and cover with water. Bring up to the boil and simmer for 1½ hours. During this time, skim off any foam that rises to the surface and top up the water as necessary to ensure everything remains covered with water.

**2** Remove the ham hock, then blend the liquid using a hand-held blender or food processor to create a smooth soup. Season the soup with salt, if needed, and black pepper.

**3** Cut the ham off the bone and return it to the soup. Serve the soup with a helping of Scone Rarebit.

Don't you just love it when two British classics come together in perfect harmony? Scones are essential to any afternoon tea and – oh my ears and whiskers – they are truly delicious when transformed into rarebit and served with Pea and Ham Soup.

# Scone Rarebit

225g (8oz) strong white flour, plus extra for dusting

1 tbsp baking powder

pinch of sea salt

50g (1¾oz) butter, diced, plus extra for greasing

2 tbsp thyme leaves

125–150ml (4–5fl oz) milk, plus extra for brushing

**For the rarebit**

15g (½oz) butter

15g (½oz) plain flour

150ml (¼ pint) ale

150g (5½oz) mature Cheddar cheese, grated

1 tsp Dijon mustard

1 tbsp Worcestershire sauce

1 free-range egg yolk

**MAKES 12**

**PREP 20** mins

**COOK 25–30** mins, plus cooling

**1** To make the scones, preheat the oven to 200°C/fan 180°C/gas mark 6. Lightly grease a baking sheet.

**2** Sift the flour, baking powder and sea salt into a bowl. Rub the butter into the flour mixture until it resembles fine breadcrumbs. Stir in the thyme leaves.

**3** Using a knife, gradually cut in just enough of the milk to make a soft dough.

**4** Roll out the dough on a lightly floured work surface to a thickness of 1cm (½in). Using a pastry cutter, stamp out 12 rounds with a diameter of 5.5cm (2¼in).

**5** Place the rounds on the prepared baking sheet. Brush with milk and bake for 12–15 minutes. Transfer the scones to a wire rack to cool.

**6** To make the rarebit, melt the butter in a saucepan and add the flour. Cook for 2 minutes, stirring, then take the pan off the heat and add the ale, stirring continuously. Return the pan to the hob and gently bring the liquid to a simmer, stirring continuously. Let it bubble away for 3 minutes, then remove the pan from the heat again and add the cheese, mustard and Worcestershire sauce. Leave the mixture to cool for a few minutes, then whisk in the egg yolk.

**7** Preheat the grill on a high setting. To assemble the rarebit, cut the scones in half, place them on a baking sheet and add a dollop of rarebit mixture on top of each half. Grill the scones for roughly 3 minutes until they are deliciously golden and bubbling.

At a gathering of girls I often find these dips to be the most popular of all the food on offer. I have got through gallons of hummus, breads and crudités at baby showers, and would simply need to remortgage my property if I were to buy them each time. Dips and breads are simple and cheap to make, and won't fail to hit the spot. Tailor the flavours to your group's tastes and don't mention how easy it is to make the flatbreads; your guests won't believe you!

# DIP DELIGHT WITH HOMEMADE FLATBREADS

## CHUNKY BEETROOT DIP

125g (4½oz) cooked vacuum-packed beetroot, grated

1 tbsp horseradish sauce

50ml (2fl oz) crème fraîche

**1** Simply mix together all the ingredients and serve!

**SERVES 6** as a trio of dips
**PREP 40** mins, plus chilling and proving
**COOK 40** mins

## Baba Ghanoush

1 large aubergine

1 tsp olive oil

2 small garlic cloves, crushed

3 tbsp tahini

1 tbsp lemon juice

60ml (2fl ¼oz) extra-virgin olive oil

salt and black pepper

**1** Preheat the oven to 200°C/fan 180°C/gas mark 4. Place the aubergine on a baking sheet, rub the 1 teaspoon olive oil over it and bake for 30–40 minutes or until the flesh is soft. Leave it to cool slightly.

**2** Carefully peel and discard the aubergine skin. Blend the flesh with the garlic, tahini, lemon juice and extra-virgin olive oil in a food processor until smooth. Season the dip to taste before serving.

## AVOCADO HUMMUS

1 avocado, peeled and stoned

210g can chickpeas, drained

½ onion, chopped

2 large garlic cloves

3 tsp lemon juice

1 tsp ground cumin

salt and black pepper

**1** Blend all the ingredients in a food processor, then place the mixture in a bowl, cover it with clingfilm and refrigerate for at least 1 hour before serving.

## FLATBREADS

½ tsp salt

1 tbsp extra-virgin olive oil

250g (9oz) plain flour, plus extra for dusting

**1** Dissolve the salt in 125ml (4fl oz) lukewarm water, then add the oil. Add the water mixture slowly to the flour, kneading the mixture until the dough is smooth. Cover with a clean, dry cloth and set aside for 30 minutes.

**2** Roll out walnut-sized pieces of the dough thinly on a floured surface into 10cm × 5cm (4in × 2in) flatbreads. Cook each piece in a dry frying pan for 3 minutes per side, then serve them with your delicious dips!

At the mention of this pudding, my mind races through the various references to fools, from the fool that accompanied King Lear on his journey across the howling heath, to the modern question "What kind of fool are you?" But the name of this delicate dessert actually comes from the French word *fouler*, meaning to press or crush, referring to the crushed fruits that are gently folded into thick cream. It is this simplicity that makes the dish shine. And as the British fool, I get to choose the berries and sing "here we go round the mulberry bush" as I dish up!

# GREAT BRITISH FOOL

**SERVES 6**

**PREP 5** mins, plus chilling

**COOK 10–15** mins

240ml (8½fl oz) whipping cream

1 tbsp icing sugar

240ml (8½fl oz) fruit compôte

**For the compôte**

450g (1lb) seasonal fruit (such as blackberries, gooseberries, mulberries or rhubarb), trimmed

30g (1oz) caster sugar

couple of splashes of elderflower or ginger cordial (optional)

**1** To make the compôte, preheat the oven to 180°C/fan 160ºC/gas mark 4.

**2** Place the fruit in a large saucepan and sprinkle with the sugar. Add enough water to just cover and gently bring the mixture to the boil, allowing the sugar to dissolve. Allow the mixture to bubble away for 10–15 minutes until the fruit has completely softened.

**3** Add the cordial, if using (elderflower works very well with gooseberries, and ginger is great with rhubarb). Check the compôte for sweetness and add more sugar if you wish. Allow the compôte to cool, then chill in the refrigerator for 30 minutes.

**4** Whisk the cream and icing sugar together until soft peaks form (it should not be too thick), then fold in the compôte. Divide the fool between 6 decorative glasses and serve.

It would be rude not to have chocolate at a mother-to-be's tea party, and these gracious, gently baked cheesecakes should extract all the right sounds from your guests. I love cooking them in old make-up sets for an elegant touch. Add a sprinkle of chocolate shavings at the end to really lift the dish.

# MiNi Baked CHOCOLATE CHEESECAKES

MAKES 6

PREP 20 mins,
plus chilling

COOK 35 mins

50g (1¾oz) dark chocolate,
plus 15g (½oz) dark chocolate, chopped into pieces,
and extra shavings to decorate

50g (1¾oz) unsalted butter

100g (3½oz) digestive biscuits, crushed

100g (3½oz) cream cheese

2 tbsp caster sugar

75ml (2½fl oz) soured cream

2 free-range eggs, beaten

1 tbsp cocoa powder

1 tsp vanilla extract

**1** Preheat the oven to 170°C/fan 150°C/gas mark 3½. Break the 50g (1¾oz) chocolate into pieces and melt it in a heatproof bowl set over a saucepan of barely simmering water, ensuring the base of the bowl doesn't touch the water below. Allow the melted chocolate to cool to room temperature.

**2** Melt the butter in a saucepan and mix in the crushed biscuits. Divide the mixture equally into 6 and press 1 portion into the bottom of each of your pretty dishes or teacups (which should be at least 1cm/½in high).

**3** Mix the cream cheese and sugar until smooth, then add the soured cream, eggs, cocoa, vanilla extract and melted chocolate. Mix well, then fold in the chopped chocolate. Pour this mixture into the dishes over the biscuit bases. Place the cups in a large baking tray and add enough water to the tray to reach halfway up the outsides of the cups. Cook for 30 minutes until firm to the touch. Chill for at least an hour, and until ready to serve.

A tasty tea cosy for a hot ginger drink! Lifting box lids to reveal what's underneath is one of life's simple pleasures. This hot-drink topper evokes that feeling and, what's more, it's delicious, crunchy and perfect to dip into your Ginger Syrup Tea (*see page 172*).

# Cinnamon Tea Cosies

**MAKES** 6
**PREP** 45 mins, plus chilling
**COOK** 12–15 mins

250g (9oz) plain flour, plus extra for dusting

1 tbsp ground cinnamon

½ tsp salt

125g (4½oz) butter, softened

100g (3½oz) caster sugar

1 tsp vanilla extract

1 free range egg, beaten

**For the topping**

4 tbsp caster sugar

½ tsp ground cinnamon

**1** Sift the flour, cinnamon and salt into a bowl, then rub in the butter until the mixture resembles breadcrumbs. Add the sugar and vanilla and mix into a stiff paste, then mix in the egg to form a dough. Knead on a lightly floured surface until smooth. Wrap in clingfilm and refrigerate for 30 minutes. Preheat the oven to 180°C/fan 160°C/gas mark 4. Line a baking sheet with nonstick baking paper.

**2** Divide the dough into 2 pieces (A and B). Roll out each piece into a large rectangle and cut it into strips about 5mm (¼in) wide. On piece A, fold every other strip all the way back over itself. Lay 1 strip from B over the area on piece A with the gaps, perpendicular to the piece-A strips, placing it quite close to the line where you folded the strips from piece A back. Now unfold the strips from piece A, laying them over the strip from piece B. Next, fold back the strips from piece A that you didn't fold last time and lay down the next strip from piece B, positioning it as close as possible to the first strip from piece B. Repeat this pattern until you have used all the strips from B and have created a lattice structure. Use a pastry cutter that is just bigger than your teacups to cut out 6 discs from the lattice. Put these onto the baking sheet. (If you have a ramekin that's the same size as your teacups, upturn it, cover it with a square of nonstick baking paper, lay the toppers over that and gently push the edges of the pastry discs over the edge of the ramekin base to create a lip – you'll need to cut your circles 2cm (¾in) larger than your teacup, in this case. You can bake the biscuits on the ramekins.)

**3** Bake for 12–15 minutes until golden brown. As soon as the toppers come out of the oven, shake over a mixture of the caster sugar and cinnamon and allow the pastry to cool.

Some may argue that this is not a traditional afternoon teacake and, actually, they would be right. With this out of the way, and copious amounts of tea to be drunk, this cake oozes zesty orange and is perfect with a cuppa! Ground almonds are my secret weapon to increase levels of scrumptiousness.

# ELDERFLOWER & ORANGE
## AFTERNOON TEACAKE

**SERVES** 10–12
**PREP** 15 mins
**COOK** 45–50 mins

175g (6oz) softened butter, plus extra for greasing

175g (6oz) golden caster sugar

3 free-range eggs

140g (5oz) self-raising flour

85g (3oz) ground almonds

½ tsp baking powder

100ml (3½fl oz) milk

**For the elderflower drizzle**

4 tbsp elderflower cordial

grated rind of 1 orange

4 tbsp white or golden granulated sugar

**1** Heat the oven to 160°C/fan 140°C/gas mark 3. Grease and line a 900g (2lb) loaf tin with a strip of nonstick baking paper that overhangs the tin.

**2** Cream the butter and sugar together with a wooden spoon or an electric whisk until light and fluffy. Beat in the eggs, flour, ground almonds, baking powder and milk until the mixture is smooth. Pour it into the prepared tin. Bake for 45–50 minutes until the cake is golden and a skewer that's inserted into the centre comes out clean.

**3** Meanwhile, heat the cordial ingredients over a medium heat for 5 minutes until the sugar dissolves and the drizzle takes on the flavour of the rind. Set aside until the cake is ready.

**4** As soon as the cake is cooked, turn it out of the tin, using the overhanging paper, onto a wire rack, prick it all over with a skewer and pour over the drizzle. The pieces of orange rind will stick to the top for a lovely burst of colour. Allow the cake to cool, then slice and serve.

Cinnamon Tea Cosies

Ginger Syrup Tea

Elderflower & Orange Afternoon Teacake

Tea for most is like a warm hug. It brings us together and opens our souls to beautiful conversations. Drinking tea during pregnancy must be done with care. Caffeinated tea should be taken in moderation, yet Ginger Tea is not only delicious but is good for nausea. So ladies, drink your pregnant heart out, and if you need something cold, add sparkling water for a ginger sizzler!

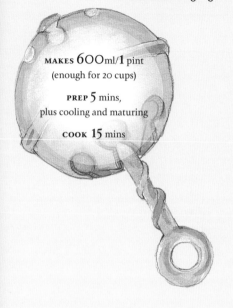

MAKES 600ml/1 pint
(enough for 20 cups)

PREP 5 mins,
plus cooling and maturing

COOK 15 mins

# Ginger Syrup Tea

100g (3½oz) fresh root ginger, unpeeled
200g (7oz) caster sugar
450ml (16fl oz) still water

**To serve cold**
sparkling water
ice cubes
lime wedges

1 Add the ginger, sugar and still water to a saucepan. Bring to the boil over a low heat, allowing the sugar to dissolve. Raise the heat and allow the mixture to bubble away for 10 minutes.

2 Remove from the heat and leave the mixture to cool to room temperature. Strain, and keep refrigerated for up to 2 weeks.

3 To serve cold, put about 2 tablespoons of the syrup in a glass and top up with sparkling water, ice and a lime wedge. Stir gently.

4 To serve hot, top up with hot water for that cosy tea! Stir gently.

Jewelled Red Jasmine Tea

Add 1 bulb of Blooming Tea Thousand Year Red (available online) to each cup of tea and top up with hot water as you go!

# HOW TO MAKE

# VINTAGE-MOTIF BABY HANGERS

Looking back at my baby pictures I can see I had some cracking outfits. My mum gave them to her best friend when she was pregnant, which I totally understood, but I would not have minded if she'd kept my cute sailor's dress, my Minnie-Mouse outfit (including ears) and my baby fur coat. If she had, I would have made these hangers and had my favourite pieces on show.

## YOU WILL NEED

✂ cream, blue and pink matt emulsion paint (use small samples sizes) ✂ paintbrush ✂ wooden hangers ✂ vintage and vintage-style printed images for the motifs ✂ craft knife ✂ cutting mat ✂ glue stick ✂ clear matt wood varnish

**1** Paint all your hangers in your chosen colours (you may need 2–3 coats). Leave the hangers to dry between coats. It will be easiest to paint 1 side at a time, leaving it to dry before turning it over to paint the other side.

**2** Cut out your motifs carefully using a craft knife. Take your time to ensure a neat finish. Then glue the motifs into place on your hangers.

**3** Allow the glue to dry for 10–15 minutes, then paint a coat of clear varnish over the hanger, including over the motif. Depending on the type of varnish used, it may look better to apply a couple of coats to achieve an even coverage. Allow to dry. Your cute vintage motif hangers are now ready to show off some very cute baby clothes.

# HOW TO CREATE THE CHEESECAKE

The 50s was the decade of the baby boomers, so we've drawn inspiration from this era for the perfect baby shower hair-do! Having kept the country going while the men were away fighting World War II, many women were spending more time at home in the 50s. Practical workplace hairstyles were abandoned in favour of fuller, softer looks. This daring, glamorous Cheesecake pin-up style reveals the neck, which is quite appealing during pregnancy, I'm told!

### YOU WILL NEED

☞ hair mousse ☞ tail comb ☞ curling tongs and Kirby grips or curl clips, or heated rollers ☞ section clips ☞ bristle brush ☞ hairspray ☞

◁ **STEP 1** Curl and set your hair (*see* page 100) using curling tongs or heated rollers. Once the hair has cooled, remove the grips or clips or rollers and part the hair across the head from ear to ear. Then divide the front section into 3 by parting the hair above both eyebrows.

◁ **STEP 2** Starting with the front section, backcomb at the hairline, working your way about halfway down the length of the hair. Then smooth the top of this section, working from the back with a bristle brush. Spray liberally with hairspray.

◁ **STEP 3** Using your fingers, roll the front section towards your face, creating a roll, and bring this forwards to meet your forehead. You have now created a fake fringe! Pin this in place at the back of the roll, then secure the hair at either side with hair grips. Use your fingers to gently fan out the hair to cover any gaps in the roll and to make it wider.

**STEP 4** Take 1 of the side sections, backcomb from behind and smooth over with the brush. Sweep the hair up and back across the head, securing with hairpins on the top of the head where the fake fringe starts. Make sure there is enough volume in this section to disguise any open edges of the front roll. Repeat on the other side.

**STEP 5** Brush the curled hair at the back off your neck and sweep it upwards. Pin it into place, forming a horizontal line with the grips all the way around the head, overlapping them to make them secure. Hairspray any flyaway hairs and smooth them with your hand.

**STEP 6** Work on the hair that has just been swept up on top of the head. Pin the curls in place, using their own structure to guide you. This bit doesn't need to be neat, as this style is soft and feminine.

As a woman, I found this chapter quite daunting to write at first. I'm not an expert at being a gentleman, nor have I ever been one. And most of our parties generally involve women. But after the publication of *The Vintage Tea Party Book*, I was happy to discover that there was a demand for the material in this chapter. The public asked! So I've taken guidance from the most dapper of the gentlemen I know and dug deep into their souls to find out what floats their handsome boats, while ensuring it all looks enchanting… the Angel way.

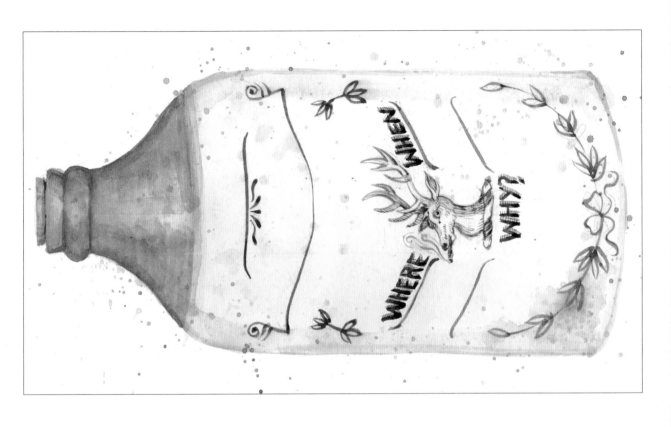

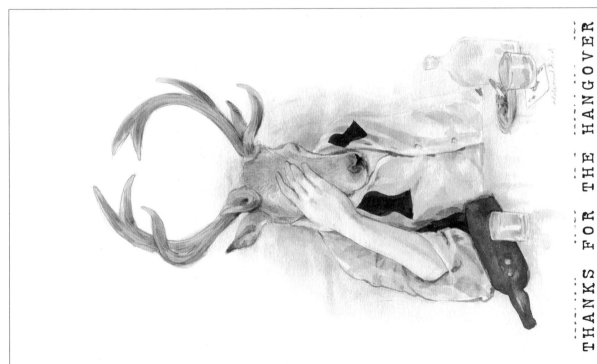

WHEN

WHY?

WHERE

THANKS FOR THE HANGOVER

Crunchy, salty, smoky, sweet and juicy.
These asparagus cigars are simply
delectable and you will want to inhale
all the flavours just like a real cigar.
The good thing is that they are much
better for you! They are better served hot
while the pastry is still crisp, but I have to
admit, they are delicious hours later, too!

# ASPARAGUS CIGARS

MAKES **12**

PREP **20** mins

COOK **10–12** mins

4 anchovies fillets in oil, drained and chopped

60ml (2¼oz) single cream

1 tbsp finely grated Parmesan cheese

1–2 tsp lemon juice, to taste

black pepper

6 sheets of 34cm × 30cm (13½in × 12in)
shop-bought filo pastry, halved

plain flour, for dusting

4 slices of prosciutto, sliced lengthways into thirds

12 asparagus spears, trimmed, blanched and drained

olive oil, for brushing

**1** Preheat the oven to 200°C/fan 180ºC/gas mark 6. Line a baking sheet
with nonstick baking paper.

**2** Grind together the anchovies, cream, Parmesan, lemon juice and some
pepper to form a paste using a pestle and mortar.

**3** Lay 1 filo rectangle on a lightly floured work surface with a short end
nearest to you. (Cover the remaining filo with a damp tea towel.) Spread
1 teaspoon of the paste onto a short end of the pastry, lay 1 piece of
prosciutto on top, then 1 asparagus spear. Brush the pastry with oil and roll
it up tightly to enclose the filling. Repeat with the remaining ingredients
to make 12 cigars. Transfer to the prepared baking sheet, leaving a 2–3cm
(¾–1¼in) gap between each, and brush with a little more oil. Bake the
cigars for 10–12 minutes until crisp and light golden. Serve immediately.

While on holiday in France, my partner and I ate an unusual steak tartare that oozed with the flavour of curry. We were shocked at how delicious it was and made it our mission to recreate it once back home. We discovered quickly that the steak's delicate flavour must be treated with respect as the star of the dish. So taste the finished dish (oh, if I must), and adjust the flavour by adding a little more of any ingredient as necessary, to get the balance just right. "Yum yum", says Dicky the Fox.

# CURRIED STEAK TARTARE

**MAKES 18**
**PREP 15 mins,**
plus optional chilling

200g (7oz) finest-quality steak, finely chopped
40g (1½oz) shallot, very finely chopped
2 tsp curry powder
2 tsp Worcestershire sauce
6 drops of Tabasco sauce
good pinch of salt and black pepper
flat-leaf parsley, to garnish

**1** Mix together all the ingredients except the parsley in a bowl, then form the mixture into 18 lozenges.

**2** Either chill, covered, for up to 2 hours, removing from the refrigerator 10 minutes before serving, or serve immediately, garnished with flat-leaf parsley leaves.

Gentlemen's Relish is a strong anchovy paste invented by an Englishman called John Osborne in 1828, who must have been pretty canny, as the recipe is still produced today under secret licence! My dad loves my version spread thinly over toast.

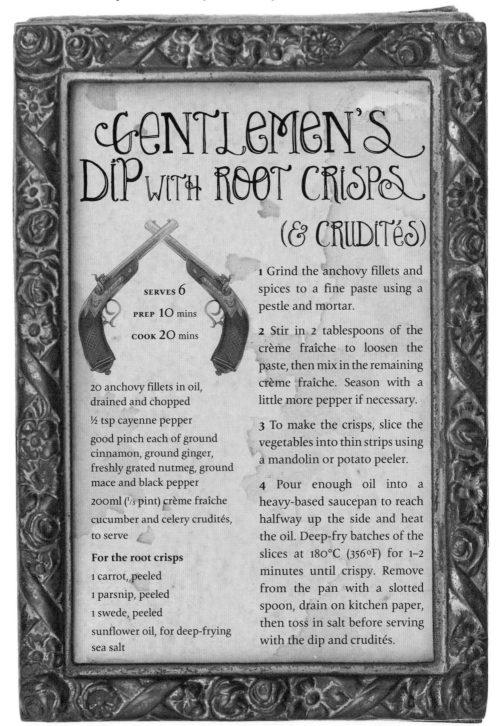

# GENTLEMEN'S DIP WITH ROOT CRISPS
## (& CRUDITÉS)

**SERVES** 6

**PREP** 10 mins

**COOK** 20 mins

20 anchovy fillets in oil, drained and chopped

½ tsp cayenne pepper

good pinch each of ground cinnamon, ground ginger, freshly grated nutmeg, ground mace and black pepper

200ml (⅓ pint) crème fraîche

cucumber and celery crudités, to serve

**For the root crisps**

1 carrot, peeled

1 parsnip, peeled

1 swede, peeled

sunflower oil, for deep-frying

sea salt

1 Grind the anchovy fillets and spices to a fine paste using a pestle and mortar.

2 Stir in 2 tablespoons of the crème fraîche to loosen the paste, then mix in the remaining crème fraîche. Season with a little more pepper if necessary.

3 To make the crisps, slice the vegetables into thin strips using a mandolin or potato peeler.

4 Pour enough oil into a heavy-based saucepan to reach halfway up the side and heat the oil. Deep-fry batches of the slices at 180°C (356°F) for 1–2 minutes until crispy. Remove from the pan with a slotted spoon, drain on kitchen paper, then toss in salt before serving with the dip and crudités.

Faggots are traditionally made of a mixture of meat offcuts shaped into a ball and wrapped in caul (pigs' stomach lining). The caul is visually the best bit, as it creates a beautiful lacy effect. If you can't get hold of caul, using thin pieces of pancetta is not a bad alternative, trust me!

# Lacy Faggots

MAKES 24
PREP 30 mins
COOK 25 mins

100g (3½oz) pigs' liver

125g (4½oz) pork belly

100g (3½oz) pork shoulder

50g (1¾oz) streaky bacon scraps

50g (1¾oz) fresh white breadcrumbs

½ onion, finely chopped

handful of chopped parsley

few sage leaves, finely chopped

small sprig of rosemary, finely chopped

pinch of ground mace

½ tsp cayenne pepper

½ tsp allspice

pinch of salt

pinch of white pepper

12 slices of pancetta

1 Preheat the oven to 180°C/fan 160°C/gas mark 4.

2 Very finely chop the pigs' liver, pork belly, pork shoulder and bacon and combine them in a bowl. Add all the remaining ingredients except for the pancetta to the meat and mix thoroughly.

3 Shape the mixture into 24 small balls, each about 3cm (1¼in) in diameter. Cut each slice of pancetta in half lengthways, then in half again widthways. Use 2 pieces of pancetta to wrap each faggot so that they cross at the top.

4 Place the faggots on a baking sheet and roast for 25 minutes or until the pancetta is crispy and the pork is cooked through.

Freshly cooked squid oozing with garlic butter and chilli will send anyone into fishy heaven. When I eat this with my dapper gentleman, he has the tentacles and I eat the body.

# Fishy Trenchermen

MAKES 8
PREP 30 mins
COOK 15–20 mins

2 × 450g (1lb) stale unsliced white farmhouse loaves

125g (4½oz) butter, melted

500g (1lb 2oz) baby squid

2 tbsp olive oil

2 garlic cloves, finely chopped

1 red chilli, finely chopped

300g (10½oz) tomatoes, deseeded and diced

grated rind and juice of 1 lime

2 tbsp chopped fresh coriander leaves

1 Preheat the oven to 180°C/fan 160°C/gas mark 4.

2 Carefully cut the crusts off the loaves, then cut each loaf into 4 cubes. Hollow out the cubes with a spoon to make 8 bread boxes.

3 Coat the bread boxes inside and out with the melted butter and place them on a baking sheet. Cook for 10–15 minutes until golden.

4 To prepare the squid, pull out the tentacles and ensure the beak has been removed. Cut the tentacles in half and cut the squid bodies into 3 or 4 small rings.

5 Heat the oil in a frying pan set over a medium heat and add the garlic. After a few seconds, add the squid, turn up the heat and flash-fry the squid for 1 minute, tossing it about the pan.

6 Add the chilli, cook for a minute, then add the tomatoes. Cook over a medium heat for 3 minutes, then add the lime rind and juice and coriander leaves.

7 Take the pan off the heat and spoon the mixture into the hollows of the bread boxes, dividing it equally. Serve immediately.

My grandpa is a dapper man. He worked hard all his life in a printing firm in East London and inspired all his children to have great work ethics. He also loves the doughnuts that my granny made for the family. I only found this out recently when researching this chapter. I never knew that when my granny used to make them for the kids, he stood by the fryer chatting so that he could steal some! If they are good enough for my grandpa Don, they are good enough for anyone!

# DOUGHNUT balls WITH
## COFFEE CREAM & CINNAMON SUGAR

MAKES 24

PREP 30 mins,
plus proving
and cooling

COOK 40–55 mins

150ml (¼ pint) milk

50g (1¾oz) butter

250g (9oz) strong white flour, plus extra for dusting

1 × 7g (¹/8oz) sachet dried yeast

125g (4½oz) caster sugar

2 free-range egg yolks

sunflower oil, for deep-frying and oiling the bowl

2 tsp ground cinnamon

**For the coffee cream**

2 large free-range egg yolks

70g (2½oz) caster sugar

½ tbsp cornflour

1 tsp vanilla extract

2 shots of strong espresso, at room temperature

200ml (⅓ pint) double cream

60ml (2¼fl oz) skimmed milk

1 Heat the milk in a small saucepan just to boiling point. Take the pan off the heat, add the butter and allow the butter to melt and the milk to cool a little. Combine the flour, yeast and 50g (1¾oz) of the sugar in a large bowl. Add the egg yolks to the milk (it should be tepid by now), then add this mixture to the dry ingredients. Combine well, then leave it to sit for a few minutes. Knead on a floured work surface for a good 15 minutes until smooth and elastic (when you prod the dough it should spring back out). Place in a well-oiled bowl, cover the dough with clingfilm and leave to rise in a warm place for a few hours until almost doubled in size.

2 Take the dough out of the bowl and knock out the air. Shape into 24 small balls, place these on a baking sheet, cover with clingfilm and leave to prove for 30–45 minutes.

3 Put at least 8cm (3¼in) oil in a deep-fat fryer or a saucepan. Fry the doughnuts in batches at 180°C/356°F for 2–3 minutes on each side until golden brown. Remove from the oil using a slotted spoon and place on kitchen paper. Allow the doughnuts to cool.

4 Mix the remaining sugar with the cinnamon in a bowl, then toss each doughnut in the mixture to coat. Place the doughnuts back on the baking sheet to allow them to cool for 30–40 minutes.

5 To make the coffee cream, mix the egg yolks, sugar, cornflour, vanilla extract and espresso in a small saucepan. Whisk until well combined, then add 2 tablespoons of the cream and heat over a medium-high heat, stirring continuously. Mix the milk with the remaining cream and add this to the pan, little by little, stirring continuously, until all the milk has been incorporated. Stir for 5–10 minutes until the mixture coats the back of a wooden spoon. Remove from the heat and let the cream cool. Set clingfilm on the surface of the cream to prevent a skin forming.

6 Put the coffee cream into a piping bag with a plain nozzle. Poke a small hole into the side of each doughnut and fill with the coffee cream.

# BRANDY SNAPS WITH RHUBARB SYLLABUB

**MAKES 12**

**PREP 30** mins,
plus cooling

**COOK 40–50** mins

vegetable oil, for oiling
the spoon (optional)

75g (2¾oz) butter

75g (2¾oz) caster sugar

3 tbsp golden syrup

75g (2¾oz) plain flour

2 tsp brandy

1 tsp ground ginger

½ tsp ground cinnamon

finely grated rind of 1 lemon

**For the rhubarb syllabub**

50g (1¾oz) granulated sugar

200g (7oz) trimmed rhubarb,
cut into 1cm (½in) lengths

generous tot of brandy

250ml (9fl oz) double cream

1 Preheat the oven to 180°C/fan 160°C/gas mark 4. Line a baking sheet with nonstick baking paper and rub vegetable oil onto the handle of a wooden spoon, or use a silicone spoon of a similar size.

2 Melt together the butter, sugar and golden syrup in a saucepan. Stir in the flour, brandy, spices and lemon rind.

3 Drop small spoonfuls of the mixture onto the prepared baking sheet, spaced well apart as they will spread in the oven. It is best to cook the snaps in 2–3 batches so you'll have time to shape them while they are still pliable.

4 Bake the snaps for 6–8 minutes. They're ready when the mixture has spread out into lacy, golden discs. Remove the snaps from the oven and leave them to cool for a minute before shaping.

5 Use the oiled wooden spoon handle to shape the brandy snaps into cylinders. Leave these on a wire rack to cool. If the snaps become too brittle to shape, return them to the oven for a minute to soften. Repeat the shaping with the remaining mixture.

6 For the rhubarb syllabub, put 50ml (2fl oz) water and the sugar in a pan and heat until the sugar dissolves. Add the rhubarb, heat until it simmers, then continue cooking for about 15 minutes until it is soft. Remove from the heat and allow to cool.

7 Add the brandy and pass the rhubarb mixture through a sieve. Whisk the cream to soft peaks, then gently fold in the rhubarb mixture.

8 Spoon the syllabub into a piping bag with a plain nozzle. Pipe into the brandy snaps just before serving.

# CHOCOLATE MINT FUDGE PIECES

1 Line the base of a 20cm (8in) square cake tin with nonstick baking paper.

2 Melt the dark chocolate with 250g (9oz) of the condensed milk and the vanilla in a heavy-based pan over a low heat, stirring continuously. Spread half the mixture over the base of the tin and chill in the refrigerator for 45 minutes or until firm. Keep the remaining chocolate mixture at room temperature.

3 In another heavy-based pan set over a low heat, melt the white chocolate with the remaining condensed milk. Stir in the peppermint extract and the food colouring, if using. Spread this over the chilled layer; chill for a further 45 minutes or until firm.

4 Reheat the reserved chocolate to soften, then spread the mixture over the mint layer. Chill for 2 hours or until firm. Cut into 40 rectangles.

**MAKES 40**

**PREP 20** mins,
plus chilling

**COOK 10** mins

350g (12oz) dark chocolate

397g can condensed milk

2 tsp vanilla extract

175g (6oz) white chocolate

1 tbsp peppermint extract

2 drops of green food colouring
(optional)

Chocolate Mint
Fudge Pieces

Doughnut Balls

Brandy snaps

A whisky sour is one of the few things other than a beer that one could ask for in order to sound over-the-top masculine, so it would be punishment not to include this recipe here. My male friends love the strong flavours of the bitters, and I do my bit by serving up these drinks in attractive old pharmacy bottles. "Honestly, it's not poison!"

# WHISKY SOUR

**SERVES 1 | PREP 5 mins**

2–4 drops of Angostura bitters
50ml (2fl oz) whisky
1 tbsp lemon or lime juice
soda water or lemonade
ice cubes

**1** Put the bitters in an old pharmacy bottle or glass and add the whisky and the lemon or lime juice.

**2** Stir the drink, then top it up with soda water or lemonade and ice cubes.

There are many tales about the invention of the Gimlet, but most include a "Dr Gimlet", a "Sailor" and a mention of the fact that this sweet-and-sour drink was invented as a cure for something. Hmm...

# BASIC GIMLET

**SERVES 1** | **PREP 1** min

50ml (2fl oz) gin
30ml (1fl oz) lime cordial
ice cubes

**1** Mix the ingredients in a shaker and serve!

# How to Make a Bow Tie

A gentleman's dapperness depends upon his discreet attention to detail. Anyone can buy a ready-made clip-on tie but, to really impress your peers, make your own. The advantage? You get to match it to your handkerchief, which may match your jacket lining, which may, in turn, match your shoes... Yes, it's all in the detail!

## YOU WILL NEED

✂ measuring tape and ruler ✂ access to a photocopier ✂ large sheet of paper ✂ pencil and thin marker pen ✂ paper and fabric scissors ✂ iron ✂ 50cm (½yd) thin iron-on interfacing ✂ 50cm (½yd) thin silky patterned fabric for the bow tie (recycling an old cravat works well) ✂ needle and thread to match your fabric ✂ sewing machine

TEMPLATE AT 25 PER CENT ACTUAL SIZE

**1** Firstly, if you don't already know your neck size, measure your neck with a measuring tape.

**2** Next, photocopy this page at 400 per cent and cut out the bow-tie template. Draw around it on a large sheet of paper, extending the central section to match your measured neck size.

**3** Iron the interfacing onto the wrong side of your chosen bow-tie fabric.

**4** Lay the template on the wrong side of the bow-tie fabric, on the interfacing, and draw around it with a thin marker pen. Cut out the shape. Repeat this process so that you have 2 pieces.

**5** Lay the 2 pieces of backed fabric on top of one another, right sides together, and tack around 3 sides of the bow tie, leaving a narrow end open. Sew the same with your sewing machine, using the edge of the pressure foot as a guide to the seam allowance, then remove the tacks.

**6** Turn the bow tie right sides out through the gap (you may wish to push a pencil into the corners of the bow tie to give them a nice point). Use a needle and thread to hand sew a tight blanket stitch over the open gap, to close it.

**7** Now simply iron your bow tie flat on a low heat and it's ready to wear!

**HOW TO TIE A BOW TIE**

STREET TEA PARTY

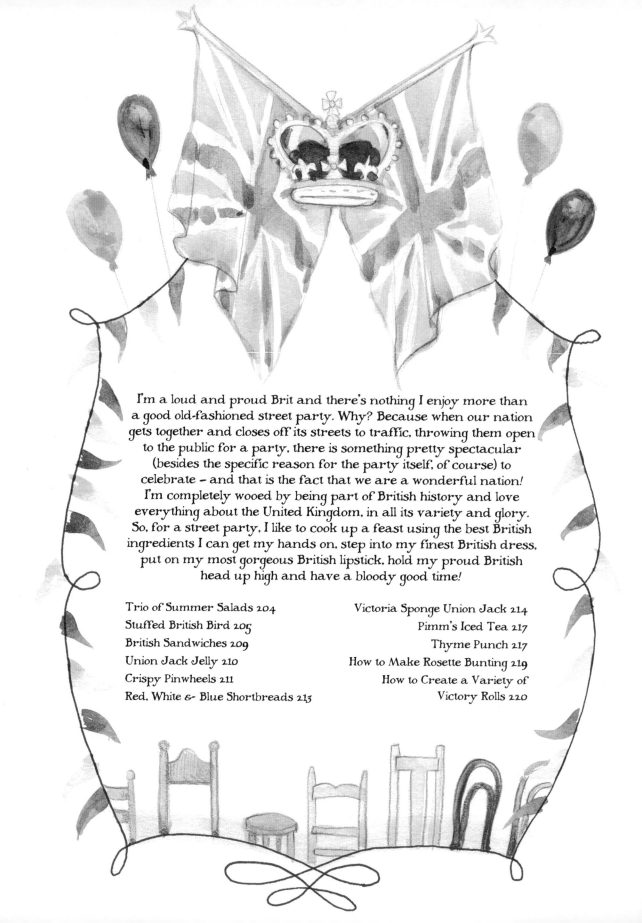

I'm a loud and proud Brit and there's nothing I enjoy more than a good old-fashioned street party. Why? Because when our nation gets together and closes off its streets to traffic, throwing them open to the public for a party, there is something pretty spectacular (besides the specific reason for the party itself, of course) to celebrate – and that is the fact that we are a wonderful nation! I'm completely wooed by being part of British history and love everything about the United Kingdom, in all its variety and glory. So, for a street party, I like to cook up a feast using the best British ingredients I can get my hands on, step into my finest British dress, put on my most gorgeous British lipstick, hold my proud British head up high and have a bloody good time!

You are invited to participate
in our

STREET PARTY

Which will be held at:

in honour of:

the party starts at:

don't be late!

Grace your trestle table with the fresh taste of summer. These are my family's simple-but-delicious salads that have fed the masses and will continue to do so! Even as grown-ups we still go to war over the last spoonful of my mum's potato salad!

# TRIO OF SUMMER SALADS

## POTATO SALAD

**PREP 15** mins | **COOK 15–20** mins

900g (2lb) new potatoes, such as Jersey Royals

salt and black pepper

1 small red onion, finely chopped

3 free-range eggs, hard boiled

5 tbsp mayonnaise

2 tbsp crème fraîche

good handful of flat-leaf parsley, chopped, plus extra to garnish

**1** Cook the potatoes in lightly salted water for 15–20 minutes until they are tender. Drain the potatoes and, when they are just cool enough to handle, slice them into rounds, quarters or squares – whichever you prefer.

**2** Mix together the onion, eggs, mayonnaise, crème fraîche, parsley and some seasoning in a large serving bowl. When the potatoes are still warm but no longer hot, add them to the mayonnaise mixture and gently combine. Serve warm or cold, garnished with parsley.

## CHERRY TOMATO SALAD

**PREP 15** mins, plus resting

450g (1lb) cherry tomatoes of various colours, halved

½ red onion, thinly sliced

salt and black pepper

3–4 tbsp good-quality extra-virgin olive oil

10 large basil leaves

**1** Place the cherry tomatoes in a large serving bowl with the red onion slices. Sprinkle over some salt and pepper and drizzle over the olive oil. Mix well and taste, adjusting the seasoning if required.

**2** Tear the basil leaves over the salad and mix gently. Leave to rest for at least 15 minutes, to allow the flavours to mingle, before serving.

## COLESLAW

**PREP 20** mins, plus chilling

300g (10½oz) white cabbage, thinly sliced

225g (8oz) carrots, coarsely grated

1 dessert apple, peeled, cored and thinly sliced

2 shallots, thinly sliced

½ fennel bulb, thinly sliced

½ tsp caraway seeds

salt and black pepper

**For the dressing**

75ml (2½fl oz) natural yogurt

1 tbsp cider vinegar

1 tsp soft light brown sugar

75ml (2½fl oz) mayonnaise

salt and black pepper

**1** Combine the yogurt, vinegar, sugar and mayonnaise in a small bowl and mix well, then season with salt and pepper.

**2** Put all the coleslaw ingredients in a large salad bowl and toss together. Pour the dressing over and toss again. Cover and refrigerate for about an hour. Season with salt and pepper just before serving.

When feeding a large party, it's important to keep an eye on costs without sacrificing quality. One of my tips is to ask your butcher to debone a good-quality chicken, so you can ensure every last piece is used up. For this recipe I stuff the chicken with butternut squash, apple, pork and sage, but you can use whatever takes your fancy. This dish is great thinly sliced and used in sandwiches, or served with salad.

# stuffed BRITISH BIRD

**SERVES** 6–8

**PREP** 20 mins, plus cooling and resting

**COOK** 1 hour 20 mins

½ butternut squash, peeled, deseeded and chopped

salt and black pepper

30g (1oz) butter

1 whole chicken (approx. 1.8kg/4lb total weight), deboned (ask your butcher to do this for you)

3 pork sausages

5 sage leaves, torn

2 tbsp olive oil

**For the apple purée**

2 dessert apples, peeled, cored and chopped

50ml (2fl oz) apple juice

**1** Preheat the oven to 180°C/fan 160ºC/gas mark 4.

**2** Cook the squash in salted boiling water for 15–20 minutes or until tender. Drain and add the butter. Mash, then season to taste. Cool.

**3** To make the apple purée, put the apples in a small pan with the apple juice and cook over a low heat for 10–15 minutes until soft. You may need to add a bit more apple juice to stop the apples drying out. Cool.

**4** Place the bird skin-side down on a chopping board, level out as much as possible, then season.

**5** Spread the squash evenly all over the chicken, then squeeze out the meat from the sausages and place it on top of the squash. Scatter the sage leaves over the sausage meat. Finally, spoon over the apple purée, then roll up the chicken and truss it with kitchen string.

**6** Brush the outside of the bird with the oil and season with salt and pepper. Place the roll in a roasting tin and cook for 45–60 minutes until golden brown and cooked through.

**7** Remove the bird from the oven and allow the meat to rest for 10 minutes before slicing.

Potato Salad

Cherry Tomato Salad

Coleslaw

Stuffed British Bird

Thank God for the Earl of Sandwich; without him we would all be eating baguettes! I love to serve classic sandwich combinations with interesting breads that complement the fillings. If I'm watching my pennies I cut them into triangles to prevent wastage, but I do like to show off by using cookie cutters, like these card-suit ones, which offer a fab way to create cute edible decoration!

**MAKES 1** sandwich of each flavour

**PREP 5** mins

# BRITISH SANDWICHES

## HAM & MUSTARD

butter, at room temperature

2 slices of brown bread

1 thick slice of ham off the bone

English mustard

**1** Butter both slices of bread on 1 side. Add the ham to 1 slice, spread some English mustard on the other slice and sandwich together. Cut out fancy shapes using cookie cutters.

## CHEESE & PICKLE

butter, at room temperature

2 slices of pumpernickel bread

1 thick slice of mature Cheddar cheese

your favourite pickle

**1** Butter both slices of bread on 1 side. Lay the cheese on 1 slice, spread some of the pickle on the other slice and sandwich together. Cut out fancy shapes using cookie cutters.

## FISHFINGER

butter, at room temperature

2 slices of white bread

3 cod fishfingers, cooked

tomato ketchup

**1** Butter both slices of bread on 1 side. Place the fishfingers on 1 slice, spread some tomato ketchup on the other slice and sandwich together. You may need to squish down the sandwich before cutting out fancy shapes using your cookie cutters.

## PRAWN COCKTAIL

1 tbsp mayonnaise

1 tsp tomato ketchup

50g (1¾oz) cooked and peeled king prawns

1 sprig of dill, leaves snipped

butter, at room temperature

2 slices of tomato bread

**1** In a small bowl, mix together the mayonnaise and tomato ketchup thoroughly. Add the prawns and a sprinkling of dill leaves.

**2** Butter both slices of bread on 1 side. Spoon the prawn mixture onto 1 slice and sandwich together with the other slice of bread. You may need to squish down the sandwich before cutting out fancy shapes using cookie cutters.

I'm no longer the five-year-old that tried to eat jelly through a straw. I'm now a grown woman who tries to. My jelly salute to the Union Flag is time-consuming to prepare, as you'll need to allow each layer to set before adding the next. However, when cooking for a large party, you'll probably need to make a few of these jellies (and I'm confident they will be a hit!), and it takes no more time to make 10 than it does to make one!

# UNION JACK JELLY

**SERVES**
6

**PREP**
45 mins,
plus cooling
and chilling

**COOK**
45 mins

**For the blueberry jelly**

½ × 12g (½oz) sachet gelatine

175ml (6fl oz) blueberry juice

100g (3½oz) blueberries

**For the coconut jelly**

½ × 12g (½oz) sachet gelatine

1 tbsp caster sugar

175ml (6fl oz) coconut milk

**For the raspberry jelly**

125g (4½oz) raspberries

1 tbsp caster sugar

½ × 12g (½oz) sachet gelatine

1 To make the blueberry jelly, place the gelatine in a small saucepan, pour over the blueberry juice and leave it to sit for 5 minutes. Set the pan over a low heat until the gelatine dissolves; do not allow the mixture to boil. Then leave the mixture to cool to room temperature. Once it has, pour it into the base of a 600ml (1 pint) jelly mould and put this in the refrigerator until the jelly has set. Once set, scatter over the blueberries.

2 Next, make the coconut jelly. Place the gelatine and sugar in a small saucepan. Pour over the coconut milk and leave it to sit for 5 minutes. Set the pan over a low heat until the gelatine and sugar dissolve; do not allow the mixture to boil. Once dissolved, allow the mixture to cool to room temperature, then pour it over the blueberries in the mould. Place in the refrigerator to set.

3 To make the raspberry jelly, place the raspberries and sugar in a heatproof bowl and cover it with clingfilm.

Rest the bowl over a pan of gently simmering water for 30 minutes so that the juices run out of the fruit.

4 Put the fruit in a jelly bag and set it over a bowl, or line a colander with a clean tea towel or a double layer of muslin and pour in the fruit, then set the colander over a bowl. Allow the juice to drain for about 20 minutes – you may need to gently press the fruit against the side of the colander with a spoon to extract all the juices. Add cold water to the raspberry juice until you have 175ml (6fl oz) liquid.

5 Pour the liquid over the gelatine in a small saucepan and leave to sit for 5 minutes. Set the pan over a gentle heat until the gelatine dissolves; do not allow the mixture to boil. Leave the mixture to cool to room temperature, then pour it over the coconut jelly in the mould. Place in the refrigerator until set. Turn out the jelly just before serving.

Making Rice Krispie cakes with my mum is one of my first memories of cooking. I remember being incredibly proud of producing something so heavenly! My seriously cute version brings a bit of the British seaside to the table. This fun recipe offers you a very playful way of getting the kids involved in the kitchen, too.

# CRISPY PINWHEELS

MAKES 8

COOK 5 mins

PREP 40 mins, plus chilling

40g (1½oz) unsalted butter, plus extra for greasing
280g (10oz) white marshmallows
150g (5½oz) puffed rice cereal (such as Rice Krispies)
red and blue edible colour spray (available online)

**1** In large saucepan, melt the butter over a low heat. Add the marshmallows and stir until they have completely melted. Take the pan off the heat.

**2** Add the puffed rice cereal to the pan. Stir until the cereal is well coated.

**3** Using a greased spatula, tightly pack the mixture into a greased baking tray that's roughly 48cm × 36cm (19in × 14¼in) to achieve a thin but dense layer. Chill in the refrigerator for 30 minutes.

**4** Spray the cereal on 1 side with the red edible colour spray, allow to dry, then remove it carefully from the baking tray. Turn it over, place it on a chopping board and spray it blue on the other side. Cut the cereal into roughly 12cm (4¾in) squares.

**5** Cut slits into each corner of each square using a sharp knife, dividing the corners into 2. Do not cut all the way to the centre of the square.

**6** Pick a corner on 1 square and fold in 1 half of it, along the slit, towards the centre of the square. Squish the tip down at the centre. Fold up half of every corner of the square, as shown overleaf, to create a pinwheel. Repeat with the remaining squares.

STREET TEA PARTY

Shortbread is a classic Scottish biscuit that has a delightful snap when broken, and we all expect it to be lovely and buttery. These little red, white and blue beauties give you no clue as to their Scottish heritage until you taste them, after which you'll be doing the Highland fling!

# Red, White & Blue Shortbreads

**MAKES** 30

**PREP** 25 mins, plus chilling

**COOK** 10 mins

150g (5½oz) unsalted butter, softened

70g (2½oz) icing sugar

150g (5½oz) plain flour, plus extra for dusting

75g (2¾oz) rice flour or cornflour

few drops of red and blue food colouring

**1** Cream the butter and icing sugar together with a wooden spoon or an electric whisk until light and fluffy. Sift in the flours and mix in. When the mixture forms a ball, knead on a lightly floured work surface for 1–2 minutes until smooth. Divide into 3 equal portions. Add a few drops of red colouring to 1 dough portion and knead until the colour is evenly distributed. Repeat with the blue colouring and another portion of dough.

**2** Divide each dough portion in half to give you 6 equal portions – 2 red, 2 blue and 2 natural. Wrap each in clingfilm and refrigerate for 30 minutes.

**3** Put the doughs on a lightly floured work surface and pat or roll each segment until it's 5mm (¼in) thick. Shape them into similar-sized rectangles.

**4** Make a stack of these rectangles on a large sheet of nonstick baking paper, starting with a red layer, followed by a blue layer and then a natural layer, then repeat the sequence to complete the stack. Cover the dough completely with the paper and wrap it up again in aluminium foil. Chill the dough in the refrigerator for at least 2 hours until firm.

**5** Preheat the oven to 150°C/fan 130°C/gas mark 2. Remove the dough from the refrigerator and cut the stack into 15 × 5mm- (¼in-) thick slices, then cut each of these in half to give you 2 squares. Place these on a baking sheet about 2cm (¾in) apart and bake on the middle shelf of the oven for 10 minutes or until just tinged with colour. Leave to cool on the tray.

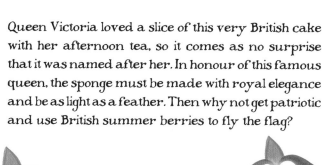

Queen Victoria loved a slice of this very British cake with her afternoon tea, so it comes as no surprise that it was named after her. In honour of this famous queen, the sponge must be made with royal elegance and be as light as a feather. Then why not get patriotic and use British summer berries to fly the flag?

SERVES
16

PREP 45 mins,
plus cooling

COOK
15–20 mins

# Victoria Sponge Union Jack

280g (10oz) unsalted butter, softened

280g (10oz) caster sugar

5 free-range eggs

280g (10oz) self-raising flour

1 tsp vanilla extract

raspberries and blueberries (approx. 400–500g/14–1lb 2oz each), to decorate

**For the buttercream**

250g (9oz) icing sugar

250g (9oz) unsalted butter, softened

1 tsp vanilla extract

**1** Preheat the oven to 180°C/fan 160°C/gas mark 4. Line the base of a 30cm × 46cm (12in × 18in) rectangular baking tray that is about 2.5cm (1in) deep with nonstick baking paper.

**2** In a food mixer, cream together the butter and sugar for about 5 minutes until pale and fluffy. With the mixer set on a slow speed, add the eggs 1 at a time, slipping in a tablespoon of the flour about halfway through to stop the mixture curdling. Sift in the remaining flour and mix until just combined, then stir in the vanilla extract.

**3** Tip the cake mixture into the prepared baking tray and spread it with a spoon or spatula to cover the base. Bake for 15–20 minutes until the top is golden and the sponge is springy to the touch. Leave to cool.

**4** Run a knife around the edges of the tin to loosen the sponge, then remove it gently from the tin.

**5** To make the buttercream, sift the icing sugar into the cleaned food mixer bowl and mix with the butter for at least 5 minutes. Once it is light and fluffy, mix in the vanilla extract.

**6** Spread the buttercream over the cake. You do not want to see any cake, as this will form the base of your flag. Then, using the picture opposite as a guide, decorate the cake with the berries to form a Union Jack.

Serving delicious drinks at large parties is a hard task without a full bar of mixologists, right? NO! Let me introduce Mr Punch. He is a big bowl of cocktail normally containing fruit, alcohol and a mixer. Of course, I like to use British flavours, but you can tailor this to your taste. My biggest tips: use lemon to preserve freshness and use homemade mixers such as cold tea to keep costs down. All that's left is to hold your teacup up and make a toast to all those present, to your loved ones and, of course, to THE QUEEN!

# PIMM'S ICED TEA

**SERVES 1**

**PREP 5 mins,** plus chilling

ice cubes

90ml (3¼fl oz) Pimm's No 1

180ml (6¼fl oz) brewed Orange Pekoe tea, chilled

1½ tsp agave syrup or honey

1½ tbsp freshly squeezed lemon juice

citrus wedges, mint sprigs, quartered strawberries and cucumber ribbons, to garnish

**1** Fill a highball glass with ice. Add the Pimm's, tea, agave syrup or honey and lemon juice and stir well. Decorate the drink lavishly.

# THYME PUNCH

**SERVES 6**

5 tsp caster sugar

35ml (1¼fl oz) freshly squeezed lemon juice

250ml (9fl oz) Hendrick's gin

leaves from 6 sprigs of thyme, very roughly chopped, plus extra to decorate

650ml (1⅛ pints) cloudy lemonade

ice cubes

**1** Pour the sugar into a jug. Add the lemon juice and gin, followed by the thyme. Top up with lemonade, stir and chill.

**2** Just before serving, add a handful of ice cubes and stir again. Decorate the punch with extra thyme.

## MEMORABLE BRITISH STREET PARTIES

| | |
|---|---|
| **1919** Peace teas | **1981** Wedding of Prince Charles and Lady Diana Spencer |
| **1935** Silver Jubilee of King George V | **2000** The Millennium |
| **1937** Coronation of George VI | **2002** Golden Jubilee of The Queen |
| **1945** VE Day | **2011** Wedding of Prince William and Catherine Middleton |
| **1951** Festival of Britain | |
| **1953** Coronation of Queen Elizabeth II | **2012** Diamond Jubilee of The Queen |
| **1977** Silver Jubilee of The Queen | |

# How to Make
# Rosette Bunting

Bunting, which is traditionally made from small triangles of leftover fabric that are sewn together, is a very effective outdoor decoration. I could probably travel the length of Britain on the amount I have made, so for something a little different, I love this take on the classic by using rosettes. It's time-consuming and a bit fiddly, but the end result is worth it! Decorate the centre with something personal or, as I have, with The Queen!

## YOU WILL NEED

✄ kettle ✄ washing-up bowl ✄ 5 regular tea bags ✄ 1m (1yd) royal blue thin cotton fabric

✄ 1m (1 yd) white thin cotton fabric ✄ 1m (1 yd) red thin cotton fabric ✄ measuring tape

✄ fabric and paper scissors ✄ sewing machine ✄ white cotton ✄ sewing needle

✄ gold card ✄ paper and access to a computer and printer ✄ glue stick and glue gun

✄ thin white rope or cord (the length depends on how much bunting you want to make)

1 First, tea stain your fabric to give it an aged look. Boil a kettle of water several times and fill your washing-up bowl, then add your tea bags and stir. Add all your fabrics to the water and leave for at least 30 minutes, then hang the fabrics to dry.

2 When the fabrics are dry, cut each piece into strips; blue strips should measure 5cm × 50cm (2in × 20in), white strips should measure 3.5cm × 50cm (3¼in × 20in), and red strips should measure 2cm × 50cm (¾in × 20in). Take 1 strip of each colour and line them up along 1 long edge. Sew along this edge to create an overlapping red, white and blue ribbon. Repeat this process with all the strips.

3 Take 1 ribbon and fold it up several times to make a concertina. Push a needle and thread through the concertina along the stitched line where the fabric is joined. To make your round rosette shape, pull tight on the thread and bend the 2 sides of the concertina round to meet each other, adding a stitch to secure. Do this with all your ribbons.

4 Now add your royal photos. First, cut out circles from your gold card – you need enough to stick onto all your rosettes. Use something round of the correct size as a template (try the bottom of a glass). Select royal images you like (you'll find a wide selection online), resize them to fit within the gold circles and print them out. Cut out these images in circles slightly smaller than your gold circles. Stick 1 image to each of the gold circles using the glue stick. Then use your glue gun to stick 1 image in the centre of each of your rosettes.

5 Now all the rosettes are complete, simply attach them to the rope or cord at regular intervals using a couple of hand-sewn stitches.

# How to Create a
# VARIETY of VICTORY ROLLS

The VE Day Victory Roll hairstyle is perhaps the most famous and well-known vintage do of them all. The most important advice for those attempting this look is to backcomb, backcomb, backcomb! Don't be afraid, as the hair gets smoothed out when you brush it through with a good-quality bristle brush. The backcombing gives the hair volume and texture, and helps you control where you place your rolls to give the style good structure.

## YOU WILL NEED

✎ hair mousse ✎ tail comb ✎ curling tongs ✎ curl clips ✎ section clips

✎ bristle brush ✎ hairspray ✎ hair grips and hairpins

◁ **STEP 1** Create a side parting. Curl and set your hair (*see page 100*) into 3 curls at the front, on one side of the parting. Use section clips to section off the hair from your crown to the front of your ear on both sides of the parting. The back of the hair can be styled in any way you like; curled, straight or pinned up in a neat chignon. We went for a soft "pageboy" curl. To achieve this look, section and curl the hair at the back using curling tongs and, while each curl is still hot, roll the hair under and pin it into place with a curl clip. Leave these curls to cool.

▷ **STEP 2** Take out the back curls once they have cooled, leaving the front 3 curls secured for the moment. Using the bristle brush, gently brush out the curls while using your hands to encourage the hair to curl under.

◁ **STEP 3** Now, using both hands, roll the backcombed side section of hair towards your parting and secure it with hair grips. Use hairpins to close up any gaps at the back of the roll – you don't want victory rolls that you can see straight through, like a telescope!

▷ **STEP 4** Repeat steps 2 and 3 on the other side. You can play around with symmetrical or asymmetrical rolls, whatever look best suits you.

◁ **STEP 5** Finally, take the front 3 curls out of clips and, using your fingers, style this section of hair into a curl with a dramatic wave. Secure it in place with hairpins and grips.

The British Summer Picnic is a rarity for most by
default. With unpredictable weather and busy lives, the
planets really do need to align for everyone to be available when
the sun has put his hat on (hip hip hip hooray) and is coming out to play.
The unspoken rules of the picnic are such that everyone brings a little
something with them. The list of necessities – food, drink, rugs, games and,
of course, kitchen paraphernalia – is quite a lot for one person alone. This
chapter celebrates the great outdoors, with recipes that make the most
not only of what's in season but also of dishes that can cope with being
transported from the kitchen to the picnic rug
and still look delectable.

# Fancy a Picnic?

## FANCY a Label?

Although the quiche is a French dish, us Brits have been making savoury custard cooked in pastry cases since the 14th century. I don't think I've ever been to a picnic where someone has not brought a quiche with them, and I think this is simply because they are so easy to make, taste great cold and travel well!

# Pea & Salmon Quiche

**SERVES** 6

**PREP** 15 mins, plus freezing and standing

**COOK** 50–60 mins

500g (1lb 2oz) shop-bought shortcrust pastry

plain flour, for dusting

300g (10½oz) cooked salmon fillet, bones and skin removed, flaked

75g (2¾oz) frozen peas

1 tsp finely grated lemon rind

1 tsp chopped dill

salt and black pepper

3 free-range eggs

200ml (7fl oz) double cream

pinch of ground nutmeg

**1** Preheat the oven to 200°C/fan 180°C/gas mark 6. Put a baking sheet in the oven. Roll out the pastry on a lightly floured work surface and use it to line the base and sides of a 23cm- (9in-) diameter loose-bottomed fluted flan tin, trimming it to fit. Prick the base with a fork. Freeze for 15 minutes or until firm, then place the flan tin on the hot baking sheet in the oven. Bake for 10–15 minutes or until golden. Remove the flan tin from the oven and reduce the oven temperature to 180°C/fan 160°C/gas mark 4.

**2** Combine the salmon, peas, lemon rind and dill in a bowl and season. Arrange the mixture inside the cooked pastry case.

**3** Beat the eggs, then add the cream, combining well. Pour this over the salmon mixture in the pastry case. Bake for 40–45 minutes or until golden and just set. Allow the quiche to stand for at least 5 minutes before serving.

The picnic is a part of British history that has inspired many cultural interpretations; think *The Wind in the Willows* (Ratty and Mole at the boating picnic), or Jane Austen's *Emma* (the ill-fated trip to Box Hill). It would therefore be a crime to leave out the British Scone on such a sunny day. You may opt for the classic sweet variety, but this savoury version is a great take on the ever-popular cheese sarnie!

# ROSEMARY SCONES
## WITH CHEDDAR CHEESE

MAKES 6

PREP 15 mins

COOK 12–15 mins

200g (7oz) plain flour, plus extra for dusting

3 tsp baking powder

75g (2¾oz) butter, plus extra for serving

good pinch of salt

1 tsp sweet paprika

½ tsp English mustard powder

1 tbsp chopped rosemary

110ml (3¾oz) cold milk, plus extra if needed and for glazing

**To serve**

Cheddar cheese

chutney

**1** Preheat the oven to 200°C/fan 180°C/gas mark 6. Line a baking sheet with nonstick baking paper. Sift the flour and baking powder into a bowl. Add the butter and cut it into the flour with a butter knife. With your fingertips, rub it in until the mixture resembles fine breadcrumbs. Add the salt, paprika, mustard powder and rosemary and combine well.

**2** Add the milk and stir, first with the butter knife, then with your hands, until just mixed. Add extra milk if there are dry bits.

**3** Place the dough on a lightly floured work surface and pat it down to roughly 1.5–2cm (⅝–¾in) thick. Cut it into 5cm (2in) rounds using a pastry cutter.

**4** Brush some milk onto the tops of your scones, then bake for 12–15 minutes. Serve with butter, Cheddar cheese and chutney.

What makes this pie a picnic pie? "The vegetable decoration!" I hear you cry. Well, sort of. It's not just the delicious pastry and robust fillings – their freezability also earns them the title of "picnic pie" (honestly, no one will know), so you get to spend less time in the kitchen. It's hard looking fabulous and making delicious food. I need every bit of help I can get!

# Picnic Pies

MAKES 6

PREP 45 mins, plus cooling and resting

COOK 1 hour

1 Heat the olive oil in a large pan set over a low–medium heat. Cook the onion and carrot for 5–7 minutes. Increase the heat and add the chicken, sweet potatoes, mushrooms and soup. When the mixture comes to the boil, reduce the heat to a simmer and check the consistency. If it is too watery, add the cornflour mixed with 1 tablespoon cold water, stirring all the time. Season, then cook for a few more minutes until the mixture thickens. Remove from the heat and set aside to cool completely.

2 Preheat the oven to 180°C/fan 160°C/gas mark 4. Lightly grease a 6-cup muffin tin (each cup should have a diameter of 7.5cm/3in and a depth of 3cm/1¼in) with lard.

3 For the pastry, sift the flour, salt and nutmeg into a warmed bowl. Heat the lard with the milk and 75ml (2½fl oz) water in a small saucepan set over a low heat until the fat has melted, then bring to the boil.

4 Make a well in the flour and drop in 1 egg yolk. Cover the yolk with a little of the flour, then quickly add the hot liquid mixture, stirring with a wooden spoon until mixed and cool enough to handle.

5 Turn out the dough onto a lightly floured board and knead it until it becomes soft and pliable. Shape the dough into a ball, put it on a warm plate and cover with an inverted bowl. Leave it in a warm place to rest for about 20 minutes.

6 Take two-thirds of the dough and cut this into 6 equal parts. (Keep the other third warm while making the pastry cases.) Roll each of these into a ball and put 1 into each of the holes in the tin. Using your thumb, quickly press each ball flat onto the base, then up the sides to the top edge. Press the pastry over the rim of the top edge; it should overlap by at least 5mm (¼in).

7 Divide the filling into 6 equal parts, then spoon these into the pie cases.

8 Roll out the remaining pastry and cut out 6 rounds using an 8cm (3¼in) pastry cutter. Using a fork, lightly beat the remaining egg yolk in a small bowl. Then, using a pastry brush, paint some of the egg yolk around the upper edges of the pastry and gently press on the lids. Use a small fork to press the rim of each lid against the top of the pie case, make a hole in the top of each pie, then glaze with the remaining yolk. Bake the pies for 40 minutes on the middle shelf of the oven. Leave them to cool on a wire rack.

1 tbsp olive oil

1 small onion, chopped

1 carrot, chopped

300g (10½oz) skinless chicken meat, deboned and cubed

1 small sweet potato, peeled and chopped

100g (3½oz) baby chestnut mushrooms, halved

400g can chicken and mushroom soup

1 tbsp cornflour (optional)

salt and black pepper

6 baby carrots with tops, to decorate

**For the pastry**

350g (12oz) plain flour, plus extra for dusting

½ tsp salt

good grating of nutmeg

115g (4oz) lard, plus extra for greasing

75ml (2½fl oz) milk

2 large free-range egg yolks

9 When cold, store the pies in an airtight container in the refrigerator; they'll keep like this for a couple of days, but bring them to room temperature before eating and garnish by sticking a little baby carrot into the hole of each pie.

Orange and fennel is an uplifting combination. The citrus from the orange and the aniseed from the fennel are so harmonious, you would think they had been playing croquet together all their lives! This is a dish I always offer to make for a picnic, as it's so quick and yummy. I transport the salads in old jars, often one per person and, depending on how much time I have, I even garnish them!

A summer picnic would not be complete without melon. My mum used watermelon for dummies, and would sit my brother and I down in front of a plate of melon slices for hours. We would demolish a whole watermelon between us. This jelly offers a far more elegant, grown-up way of eating melon; it screams out summer and it looks stunning served in old teacups.

# ORANGE & FENNEL
## PICNIC JARS

½ tsp salt

3 oranges, peeled and thinly sliced

1 tbsp olive oil

1 large fennel bulb

½ red onion, thinly sliced

black pepper

1 tsp balsamic vinegar

MAKES 4

PREP 15 mins

**1** Sprinkle the salt over the orange slices and drizzle with the olive oil. Put these aside while you are preparing the fennel to allow the salt to bring out the citrus juices.

**2** Quarter the fennel bulb, then thinly slice it, reserving some of the fronds for garnishing. Toss the fennel slices with the orange and red onion slices and season the mixture with pepper.

**3** Drizzle the salad with the balsamic vinegar and toss it again. Divide the salad between 4 jars, scatter over some snipped fennel fronds to garnish, then secure the lids ready for your picnic.

# WATERMELON &
## CANTALOUPE JELLY

½ cantaloupe melon (approx. 1.5kg/3lb 5oz), halved and deseeded

1 wedge of seedless watermelon (approx. 1kg/2lb 4oz)

2 × 12g (½ oz) sachets gelatine

750ml (1⅓ pints) apple juice

60ml (2¼fl oz) honey

2 tbsp small mint leaves

SERVES 6

PREP 15 mins, plus cooling and chilling

COOK 5 mins

**1** Scoop out the cantaloupe and watermelon with a melon baller, divide the balls between 6 teacups (or ramekins, for picnic portability) and set aside.

**2** In a medium saucepan, cover the gelatine with the apple juice and 250ml (9fl oz) water and leave it to stand for 5 minutes. Set the pan over a low heat, allowing the gelatine to dissolve; do not let it boil. Turn off the heat and stir in the honey until dissolved, then stir in mint leaves. Allow the mixture to cool to room temperature, then pour the cooled liquid over the melon and place the teacups or ramekins in the refrigerator for about 3 hours until set.

After this picnic chapter, you will have no fear about making pastry in your sleep! These sweet Butter & Walnut Tarts are mouthfuls of nutty heaven. Making this recipe is basically a show-off way of bringing the nuts along.

# BUTTER & WALNUT TARTS

**MAKES 6**

**PREP 15** mins, plus chilling

**COOK 18–20** mins

**For the pastry**

175g (6oz) plain flour, plus extra for dusting

50g (1¾oz) cocoa powder

50g (1¾oz) icing sugar

pinch of salt

140g (5oz) butter, chilled and cubed, plus extra for greasing

3 free-range egg yolks

**For the filling**

75g (2¾oz) butter, softened

100g (3½oz) soft light brown sugar

1 tsp vanilla extract

1 large free-range egg, beaten

125ml (4fl oz) liquid glucose

60g (2¼oz) walnuts, finely chopped

**1** Preheat the oven to 190°C/fan 170°C/gas mark 5. Grease a flexible 6-cup muffin tin or a standard 6-cup muffin tin lined with foil tart cases.

**2** To make the pastry, combine the flour with the cocoa powder, icing sugar and salt in a food processor. Blend in the butter until the mixture resembles coarse breadcrumbs. Mix in the eggs and blend to form a ball. Wrap the dough tightly in clingfilm and chill in the refrigerator for 30 minutes.

**3** Roll out the dough on a lightly floured work surface into a thin sheet. Stamp out 6 × 10cm (4in) rounds with a pastry cutter and use these to line the muffin cups or foil tart cases.

**4** For the filling, cream the butter with the sugar and vanilla extract. Beat in the egg and the liquid glucose. Spoon the nuts into the prepared pastry cases. Divide the rest of the filling between the pastry cases, ensuring none is more than two-thirds full.

**5** Bake the tarts for 18–20 minutes or until the filling is golden and bubbly.

A cobbler is halfway between a crumble and a pie. I love it because you can use your sweet juicy garden fruit for the filling, which can sometimes be quite sharp but, topped with a sweet crunchy cobbler, it is summer lovin' in a clip-top jar.

# RHUBARB COBBLER
## IN a JAR

**SERVES** 6

**PREP** 20 mins, plus cooling

**COOK** 20 mins

### For the filling

250g (9oz) trimmed rhubarb, chopped into 1cm (½in) pieces

100g (3½oz) caster sugar

½ vanilla pod

grated rind and juice of ½ orange

### For the cobbler

100g (3½oz) self-raising flour

2 tbsp polenta

50g (1¾oz) caster sugar, plus extra for sprinkling

¼ tsp bicarbonate of soda

¼ tsp salt

60g (2¼oz) butter, melted

75ml (2½fl oz) buttermilk

½ tsp vanilla extract

**1** Preheat the oven to 180°C/fan 160°C/gas mark 4.

**2** For the filling, place the rhubarb in a large bowl with the sugar. Split open the vanilla pod and scrape out the seeds into the bowl. Add the orange rind and juice. Mix well and divide the mixture evenly between 6 clip-top jars.

**3** To make the cobbler, combine the flour, polenta, sugar, bicarbonate of soda and salt in a large bowl. In a small bowl, whisk together the melted butter, buttermilk and vanilla extract. Add the wet ingredients to the dry ingredients and stir to combine with a rubber spatula.

**4** To assemble the cobbler, divide the dough into 6 equal pieces and place each in a jar on top of the rhubarb mixture. Sprinkle each mound of dough with some sugar. Place the jars in a baking tray and add hot water to the tray until it reaches halfway up the outsides of the jars. Bake for about 20 minutes until the filling is bubbling and the cobblers are golden brown on top and cooked through. Cool on a wire rack for 20 minutes before serving or, if you're planning to take them somewhere, allow them to cool until just sort-of warm before putting on the lids.

When plums arrive, the holiday season starts. The decedent sweet almond frangipane and the fruity plum in this dish could be considered a twist on the classic Bakewell tart. This dessert is on my list of all-time favourites and works well with cherries, pears, peaches, apples and berries – in fact, every type of fruit. Don't be stingy on the frangipane, though; you want people to close their eyes in delight when eating these!

**PREP 20** mins, plus chilling

**BAKE 30–40** mins

**MAKES 6**

# FRANGIPANE & PLUM TARTS

### For the pastry

200g (7oz) plain flour, plus extra for dusting

15g (½oz) caster sugar

100g (3½oz) butter, chilled and cubed, plus extra for greasing

1 free-range egg

### For the frangipane

50g (1¾oz) unsalted butter, softened

50g (1¾oz) muscovado sugar

½ free-range egg

50g (1¾oz) ground almonds

½ tsp almond extract

### For the tart filling

3 ripe plums, stoned and cut into 1cm (½in) slices

**1** To make the pastry, sift the flour into a large bowl and add the sugar. Tip the cubed butter into the bowl and then rub between your fingertips until the mixture resembles fine breadcrumbs.

**2** In a small bowl, beat the egg with 2 tablespoons iced water. Pour this into the flour mixture and slowly bring the ingredients together with your hands to form a dough, being careful not to overwork it. Add extra iced water if required.

**3** Knead the dough gently on a lightly floured work surface, then wrap it in clingfilm and chill in the refrigerator for at least 30 minutes until firm.

**4** To make the frangipane, cream the butter and sugar together with a wooden spoon or an electric whisk until light and fluffy. Stir in the egg. Add the ground almonds and almond extract and mix well until everything is combined. Set aside.

**5** Preheat the oven to 180°C/fan 160°C/gas mark 4. Roll out the dough thinly on a lightly floured work surface. Use the dough to line 6 individual tartlet tins that are 8cm (3¼in) in diameter. Trim away any excess. Line each tin with nonstick baking paper and fill it with baking beans. Put the tins on a baking sheet and bake for 12 minutes. Remove the paper and beans and bake for a further 5 minutes. Allow to cool.

**6** Spoon the frangipane into the tart cases so that it reaches roughly halfway up the sides. Smooth over the surfaces with a spatula and cover the frangipane evenly with the plum slices.

**7** Bake the tarts for 15–20 minutes or until the pastry is crisp and golden brown and the fruit is tender. Remove the tarts from the oven and serve immediately or allow to cool and serve at room temperature.

THE COMMON TIGER

This ambrosial drink makes you feel like you are swallowing summer. It's light, sweet and calming. It also works very well with a dash of vodka, for an adult kick!

# CHAMOMILE COOLER

50g (1¾oz) dried chamomile flowers

2 tbsp dried lemon verbena leaves

50ml (2fl oz) honey

ice cubes

**SERVES** 6

**PREP**
**10** mins,
plus steeping
and cooling

**1** In a large saucepan set over a high heat, bring 1.2 litres (2 pints) water to the boil. Take the pan off the heat and stir in the chamomile flowers and lemon verbena leaves. Cover the pan and allow the mixture to steep for 10 minutes.

**2** Meanwhile, place a large sieve lined with muslin or damp kitchen paper over another saucepan or heatproof bowl. Strain the tea through the muslin, pressing on the herbs with the back of a wooden spoon to extract all the liquid.

**3** Stir in the honey until it dissolves, then leave the tea for about 1 hour to cool completely. Fill 6 tall glasses with ice cubes, pour the tea over the ice and serve immediately.

I'm not a lover of anything beer-flavoured, but give me sunshine and lemonade and my taste buds must change! This shandy has a bit of a Mexican twist; it's almost a beer cocktail! Old milk bottles (which your family are bound to have) make great glasses and stop the insects from getting drunk!

# SUMMER SHANDY

4 tbsp sea salt

juice of 6 limes, squeezed lime shells reserved

crushed ice

2 litres (3½ pints) Mexican lager, such as Corona

100ml (3½fl oz) lemonade

Tabasco or Worcestershire sauce, to serve (optional)

SERVES 6

PREP
10 mins

**1** Pour the salt onto a plate. Wipe the tops of 6 glass bottles (each with a minimum capacity of 360ml/12½fl oz) with the lime shells, then dip them into the salt to leave a salt rim.

**2** Put some crushed ice into a large jug, then add the lime juice and lager. Finish with a dash of lemonade and a few drops of Tabasco or Worcestershire sauce, if you like. Pour the drink through a funnel into the prepared bottles.

# How to Make a
# Headscarf Blanket

Good ideas are born out of need. I've always wanted a stylish picnic blanket, but never found one. Gingham just does not float my boat. What does, however, are the bright and energetic headscarves that I continually pick up for next to nothing! Can you see where I'm going with this?

## YOU WILL NEED

❋ heavyweight iron-on interfacing (enough to cover the wrong side of each scarf)

❋ 4 square headscarves of the same size that work together as a set ❋ iron

❋ fabric scissors ❋ sewing machine ❋ thread to match scarves and binding

❋ calico (enough to cover the same area as all 4 scarves when sewn together) ❋ pins

❋ bias binding tape (enough to bind the edges of all 4 scarves when sewn together,

so measure 1 edge of a scarf and multiply by 8)

**1** Firstly, iron a sheet of interfacing onto the wrong sides of each of your headscarves, then cut round the edges.

**2** Take 2 scarves and lay them on top of one another, right sides together. Sew along 1 side to join. Repeat this with the other 2 scarves. You should now have 2 sets of 2 scarves sewn together. You now need to use the same technique to join these pieces to make a square, so that all 4 pieces are joined together like patchwork.

**3** Cut out a piece of calico the same size as your patchwork square. Lay your patchwork on top of the calico, right sides facing out, and pin into place. Now sew all the way around the edge, using

the edge of the pressure foot as a guide to the seam allowance, joining the calico to the back of your patchwork. (Make sure your fabrics are ironed flat before you start sewing.)

**4** Now to finish the edges. Take the end of your binding and fold the tape in half around the edge of your blanket at a corner. Begin slowly sewing it in place, folding and positioning it as you go. When you get to another corner, go very slowly around it and ease the tape around the corner. When you have gone all the way around, cut off the excess tape and tidy the rough ends of the tape by turning them under and finishing with a couple of hand stitches.

# HOW TO CREATE THE
# NATTY CAT EARS TURBAN

If you want an authentically vintage but fuss-free hair-do for your picnic tea party, look no further than the turban. Known by the French as *Cache Misère* (which means to "camouflage misery"), the turban is perfect for unpredictable weather and, of course, bad hair days! This way of wearing the turban is from the 40s and looks just as stylish now as it did then.

## YOU WILL NEED

✑ long scarf  ✑ Kirby grips

▷ **STEP 1** Fold your scarf in half into a triangle, then wrap it around your head. Tightly knot it at the front of your head. Tuck the triangle at the end of the scarf under the knot.

◁ **STEP 2** Take 1 of the ends of the scarf and roll it inwards towards the knot.

◁ **STEP 3** Tuck this end into the turban at the front edge, shaping it to form a "cat's ear". Repeat on the other side. Secure the scarf in place with a Kirby grip and smile!

GUY FAWKES TEA PARTY

Remember, remember the 5th of November?
I certainly do.

I remember my mum shouting at me to stay away from the fireworks and to be careful of the sparklers, and our cat being petrified of the noise. And I remember the FOOD. Food that warms you to the cockles of your heart – sausages, soup, cheesy bread, pie, toffee apples, toffee bananas, parkin pudding, marshmallows, hot chocolate and warm cider.

In my teenage years I began to understand the history behind the celebration, which gave meaning to the occasion. But, really, I could not wait for it to arrive so that I could write my name in the air with my sparkler and eat all this delicious food till I popped!

It's safe to say that the sausage sandwich is a Bonfire Night staple. Easy to make and juicy to eat, it ticks all the right boxes. But for the exhibitionist in you, this just might not be elaborate enough (gosh, I wish I was not such a show-off). Be generous with the filling when you prepare this dish – the juicy sausage and onions need to be the star!

# Sausage & Onion Cups

### For the bread

450g (1lb) strong white flour, plus extra for dusting

2 tsp dried yeast

2 tsp granulated sugar

1½ tsp salt

15g (½oz) butter, plus extra for greasing

milk, for glazing

1 tbsp sesame seeds, for sprinkling

vegetable oil, for oiling

### For the filling

15g (½oz) butter

1 onion, halved and thinly sliced

½ tsp granulated sugar

12 cocktail sausages

**MAKES 6**

**PREP** 35–40 mins, plus proving

**COOK** 35 mins

1 Grease 6 small china sugar bowls or teacups on the inside with some butter.

2 For the filling, melt the butter in a large, deep frying pan set over a low heat and add the onion. Cover and cook gently for about 10 minutes until the onion has softened. Remove the lid, add the sugar, then cook for a further 10 minutes, stirring, until all of the liquid has evaporated and the onion has turned golden.

3 To make the bread, place the flour, yeast, sugar and salt in a large bowl and rub in the butter with your fingertips. Add 225ml (8fl oz) lukewarm water and mix to a soft dough.

4 Turn out the dough on a lightly floured work surface and knead it by folding it towards you, then pushing down and away from you with the heel of your hand. Give the dough a quarter turn and repeat the action. Knead for about 10–15 minutes until it is smooth, elastic and no longer sticky.

5 Place the dough in a bowl and cover with clingfilm. Leave somewhere warm for 1–1½ hours or until doubled in size. Then remove it from the bowl and gently knock the air out of it. Cut it into even-sized pieces and place a piece in each of the prepared bowls or teacups, which should be placed on a baking tray. Glaze with milk and sprinkle with the sesame seeds.

6 Place the tray of bowls or cups inside a large oiled plastic bag and leave it in a warm place to prove for about 45–60 minutes. The dough is ready if, when prodded on the side, the indentation remains.

7 Preheat the oven to 220°C/fan 200°C/gas mark 7. Gently prise a hole in the middle of each ball of dough and fill it with 2 sausages and some onion mixture.

8 Bake on the middle shelf of the oven for about 15 minutes, depending on the size of your bowls or teacups, or until the bread is browned and sounds hollow when tapped.

Soup is a friend on any cold day and is perfect to warm your heart and your hands! With pumpkins lining every street around this time of the year, it would be crazy not to celebrate this winter vegetable, which is complemented perfectly by a bit of spice. This soup is best made the day before, leaving you more time to get ready and position your winter beret on Guy Fawkes Night.

# SPICY PUMPKIN SOUP

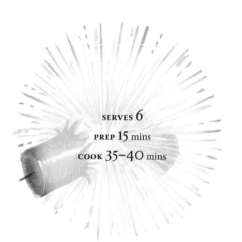

**SERVES** 6
**PREP** 15 mins
**COOK** 35–40 mins

1 tbsp vegetable oil

1 red onion, chopped

2 garlic cloves, crushed

½ tsp ground coriander

½ tsp ground cumin

½ tsp chilli powder, or to taste

1kg (2lb 4oz) pumpkin, peeled, deseeded and chopped into medium-sized pieces

1 litre (1¾ pints) chicken or vegetable stock

90ml (3¼fl oz) double cream

black pepper

**To serve**

crème fraîche

chopped chives

Rustic Bonfire Bread (*see* page 254)

**1** Heat the oil in a saucepan and cook the onion over a medium heat for 3–4 minutes. Add the garlic, coriander, cumin and chilli and cook for 1 minute more.

**2** Add the pumpkin and stock to the saucepan, bring to the boil, then simmer for 20–30 minutes or until the pumpkin is tender. Remove the pan from the heat and set it aside to allow the contents to cool slightly.

**3** Process the pumpkin and the cooking liquid in batches in a food processor or blender until smooth.

**4** Return the soup to a clean saucepan, stir in the cream, season to taste with pepper and cook over a medium heat, without boiling, until heated.

**5** Serve with a swirl of crème fraîche, a sprinkling of chives and Rustic Bonfire Bread.

My Bonfire-Night secret weapon is this quick bread. Think of it as a bread cake. Mix the ingredients together with a delicate touch, then watch it turn into something delicious in the oven! It happens to taste sublime with Spicy Pumpkin Soup (*see page 252*), or maybe you'd like to use it to make sausage sandwiches, or you could simply eat it toasted with butter.

# RUSTIC BONFIRE BREAD

**MAKES** 8 rolls

**PREP** 20 mins

**COOK** 40 mins

1 tsp olive oil

1 red onion, finely chopped

150g (5½oz) wholemeal plain flour

50g (1¾oz) fine or pinhead oatmeal

200g (7oz) plain white flour, plus extra for dusting

2 tsp cream of tartar

1 tsp bicarbonate of soda

1 tsp salt

1 tsp caster sugar

½ tsp English mustard powder

30g (1oz) butter, melted

300ml (½ pint) milk, at room temperature

175g (6oz) mature Cheddar cheese, coarsely grated

leaves from 1 sprig of rosemary, chopped

leaves from 1 sprig of thyme

85g (3oz) sunblush tomatoes, chopped

**1** Heat the oil in a frying pan, add the onion and sauté over a low heat for about 7–10 minutes until softened. Remove the pan from the heat and set it aside.

**2** Heat the oven to 190°C/fan 170°C/gas mark 5. Sift the dry ingredients into a large bowl and make a large well in the centre. Combine the melted butter and milk, then pour the mixture into the well. Mix to a soft dough.

**3** Add most of the Cheddar, the herbs, onion and the tomatoes to the dough, then gently knead on a lightly floured work surface to combine. Divide the dough into 8 lumps of equal size and shape them into rough rounds that are 2 finger-widths deep.

**4** Place the pieces of dough side by side on a floured baking sheet, scatter the remaining Cheddar over the top of them, then bake them for 30 minutes until the rolls are golden brown and the cheese is bubbling. Cool on a wire rack and eat while warm.

This dish is my personal favourite winter warmer. I love the gentle flavours of the sweet leek, the smokiness of the haddock and the richness that the cream brings, all topped with mouthfuls of silky cheesy potato. It can't help but make people smile.

# SMOKED HADDOCK & LEEK PIE WITH A CHEESY MASH TOPPING

**SERVES 6**

**PREP 25 mins**

**COOK 1 hour**

6 haddock fillets, about 115g (4oz) each

600ml (1 pint) whole milk

1 bay leaf (optional)

50g (1¾oz) butter

2 leeks, trimmed, cleaned and sliced

50g (1¾oz) plain flour

salt and black pepper

**For the cheesy mash topping**

4 large potatoes, peeled and cut into quarters

15g (½oz) butter

100ml (3½fl oz) milk

salt and black pepper

100g (3½oz) Cheddar cheese, grated

**1** Place the haddock fillets in a large saucepan set over a low–medium heat, cover with the milk and add the bay leaf, if using. Allow the milk to slowly come to the boil, then turn off the heat. Place a lid on the pan and leave the fish to sit in the hot milk for about 7 minutes. Remove the fish and flake it. Reserve the milk for later, removing the bay leaf, if using, at this stage.

**2** Meanwhile, make the cheesy mash topping. Boil the potatoes until tender, then drain. Add the butter and milk and mash with a potato masher. Season to taste. Add the grated Cheddar and gently mix in.

**3** Preheat the oven to 200°C/fan 180°C/gas mark 6.

**4** Heat the butter in a pan set over a medium heat. Add the leeks and fry for 5–6 minutes until soft. Add the flour, stir well and cook for a further 1–2 minutes. Remove the pan from the heat and gradually stir in the milk that was used to poach the haddock. Return the pan to the heat, gently bring up to a simmer, stirring well, and cook for about 5 minutes until the sauce has thickened. Season with salt and pepper.

**5** Place half the sauce in individual heatproof bowls. Put the haddock fillets on top of the sauce, then spoon over the remainder. Top each bowl with cheesy mash. Place the bowls on a baking sheet and bake for 25–30 minutes until the topping is golden brown.

Eton Mess is a British tradition. I love telling the story of how the students of Eton dropped a pavlova to create a mess and the name of this famous pudding was born. It is normally made with fresh summer berries to break up the sweetness of the cream and meringue. But when it's cold and wintery, if you're like me, you'll want something scrumptiously sweet inside you, and on these occasions, this is your Mr Perfect – Dr Banana Eton Mess.

# BANANA-ETON MESS
## WITH CARAMELIZED BANANA SAUCE

**SERVES 6**

**PREP 25** mins, plus cooling

**COOK 7** mins

150ml (¼ pint) double cream

150ml (¼ pint) crème fraîche

3 small shop-bought meringues

**For the caramelized banana sauce**

100g (3½oz) unsalted butter

100g (3½oz) soft dark brown sugar

3 bananas, sliced

100ml (3½fl oz) double cream

1 tbsp dark rum

**To decorate**

1 banana, sliced

chopped mixed nuts (optional)

1 For the sauce, place the butter and sugar in a saucepan and cook over a medium heat, stirring continuously, until the mixture darkens and caramelizes. Add the bananas, rum and the 100ml (3½fl oz) double cream and stir for a few minutes until the bananas have softened. Leave to cool.

2 In a separate bowl, whisk the 150ml (¼ pint) cream together with the crème fraîche until soft peaks form.

3 Break up the meringues using a rolling pin. Stir most of the broken meringues into the cream mixture, reserving a little for decorating.

4 To serve, spoon the meringue-cream mixture into the bottom of 6 decorative glasses. Add a layer of the caramelized banana sauce. Repeat the process with the remaining ingredients, reserving some of the banana sauce to top. Decorate each Eton Mess with banana slices, a sprinkling of chopped nuts, if using, and the remaining meringue and sauce.

In 1908 William W Kolb invented the toffee apple. This humble candy maker was experimenting with red candy and apples during the festivities and wake of the annual apple harvest season, and the rest, as they say, is sweet history. Don't just stop at these colours, though; try blue, pink, orange and even purple. You're getting the gist.

# Toffee Blackballs

MAKES 6
PREP 15 mins, plus cooling
COOK 30 mins

6 unwaxed dessert apples

6 wooden twigs or sticks, trimmed and sprayed with gold or silver edible lustre (available online)

260g (9¼oz) granulated sugar

½ tsp white wine vinegar

few drops of blackberry-flavoured oil (available online)

¼ tsp red food colouring

¼ tsp black food colouring

1 Cover a baking sheet with a large sheet of nonstick baking paper.

2 Remove the stems and any leaves from the apples. Make a little hole in the bottom of each apple for the twigs or sticks. Set aside.

3 Combine 125ml (4fl oz) water with the sugar and vinegar in a small heavy-based saucepan set over a medium heat. Slowly dissolve the sugar, then bring the mixture to the boil.

4 Heat the mixture to 150°C (302°F) on a sugar or jam thermometer. (If you don't have a sugar or jam thermometer, test the mixture after 20 minutes of cooking by dropping a spoonful into a cup of cold water. The mixture should become hard and will crack when you tap it with the back of a metal spoon.)

5 Remove the syrup from the heat and, when the mixture has stopped bubbling, stir into it the flavoured oil and red food colouring. Allow it to sit for a little while to thicken up a touch. Dip 3 apples, one by one, into the syrup, swirling them around to ensure they are evenly coated.

6 Remove each apple from the syrup with a slotted spoon and hold it above the pan to drain off the excess syrup. Place them on the prepared baking sheet, stick a twig or stick into the hole in each apple and leave for about 20 minutes to cool and harden.

7 After you've done 3 apples, add the black colouring to the syrup, then repeat the dipping process. If your syrup thickens or cools too much, simply reheat it briefly before proceeding. Allow the apples to cool completely before serving.

Bonfire Night was special in my house. The men would bond over failing to light the fireworks, while the women would bond in the kitchen over sweet treats my mum's girlfriends had brought. I don't remember a 5th of November with no Parkin cake, ginger cake, sticky pudding, chocolate brownies or marshmallows to toast. Here are my sweet twists that meld together all I remember.

# PARKIN STICKY PUDDINGS WITH BRANDY CREAM

100g (3½oz) self-raising flour

1 tsp ground ginger

good pinch of mixed spice

pinch of salt

30g (1oz) pinhead oatmeal

150g (5½oz) soft dark brown sugar

100g (3½oz) butter

100g (3½oz) golden syrup

60g (2¼oz) black treacle

1 tbsp milk

1 large free-range egg

50g (1¾oz) stem ginger in syrup (approx. 4 pieces), chopped

**For the brandy cream**

100ml (3½fl oz) whipping cream

1 tbsp icing sugar

2 tbsp brandy

**MAKES 6**

**PREP 15** mins, plus cooling

**COOK 25–30** mins

1 Preheat the oven to 180°C/fan 160°C/gas mark 4. Sift the flour, spices and salt into a bowl. Stir in the oatmeal and sugar and make a well in the centre.

2 Meanwhile, melt the butter, golden syrup and treacle gently, whisking to emulsify, then remove from the heat and leave to cool a little. Mix this into the flour mixture with a wooden spoon. Beat the milk and egg together and mix into the mixture. Fold in the ginger.

3 Pour the mixture into individual pudding basins and bake for 20–25 minutes until the mixture is still slightly soft to the touch. Leave to cool for 30 minutes before turning out.

4 For the brandy cream, whip the cream and sugar together until soft peaks form, then fold in the brandy.

# GUY "FORKS" MARSHMALLOW BROWNIES

200g (7oz) dark chocolate

250g (9oz) butter, cubed

250g (9oz) dark muscovado sugar

4 free-range eggs

185g (6½oz) plain flour, sifted

35g (1¼oz) cocoa powder, sifted

¼ tsp baking powder

2 tsp ground cinnamon

150g (5½oz) marshmallows, chopped

**MAKES 16**

**PREP 10** mins

**COOK 55** mins– **1** hour **5** mins

1 Preheat the oven to 160°C/fan 140ºC/gas mark 3. Then line a 20cm (8in) square cake tin with nonstick baking paper.

2 Break the chocolate into pieces and melt it with the butter in a heatproof bowl set over a saucepan of barely simmering water, ensuring the base of the bowl doesn't touch the water below. Allow to cool slightly.

3 Place the sugar, eggs, flour, cocoa powder, baking powder and cinnamon in a bowl. Add the chocolate mixture and mix until combined. Fold in the marshmallows and pour the mixture into the prepared baking tin. Bake for 50–60 minutes or until a skewer inserted into the centre of the cake comes out clean. Allow to cool slightly in the tin before slicing into 16 bite-sized pieces. Pierce a cocktail fork onto the top of half of the bites and arrange them in a chequerboard fashion.

If you are all to brave the great outdoors on Bonfire Night, the drinks you intend to serve up to your friends must be warm. Hot chocolate is a classic choice but, made with real chocolate, it's a no-brainer for adults (with, maybe, a dash of sweet liqueur) and children alike. Spicy Hot Perry, on the other hand, is lighter and spicier. I wonder what Guy Fawkes was drinking while guarding the gunpowder? Here's to Guy… for being caught and not blowing up parliament!

# DELICIOUS HOT CHOCOLATE

SERVES 6
PREP 5 mins
COOK 5 mins

1.2 litres (2 pints) milk

300ml (½ pint) double cream

200g (7oz) dark chocolate, broken into pieces, plus extra grated, to serve

dash of orange liqueur for each of the grown-ups

**1** Place the milk, cream and chocolate in a saucepan. Bring gently to the boil, whisking until smooth.

**2** Serve in 6 individual cups, adding a dash of orange liqueur and a little grated chocolate to each.

# SPICY HOT PERRY

SERVES 6
PREP 2 mins, plus steeping
COOK 10 mins

1.5 litres (2¾ pints) perry (pear cider)

3 tsp soft dark brown sugar

2 cinnamon sticks, plus extra to decorate

4 cloves

4 black peppercorns

4 allspice berries

**1** Put all the ingredients into a saucepan and simmer over a medium heat for 5 minutes. Take the pan off the heat and leave the mixture to steep for at least 20 minutes. Reheat, then strain and serve. Decorate each glass with a cinnamon stick.

# How to Make Bonfire Mittens

What do you do when a well-loved old woollen jumper tragically dies? Felt it to make a cosy pair of stylish bonfire mittens, of course! To felt it, simply wash the jumper on a hot cycle with plenty of detergent and allow to dry.

**YOU WILL NEED**

✄ access to a photocopier ✄ piece of A4 paper ✄ paper and fabric scissors ✄ felted woollen jumper ✄ pins ✄ needle and thread to match jumper

**1** Use a photocopier to enlarge the mitten template, below, at 400 per cent and cut it out. Position the hand template with its straight edge aligned with the ribbed bottom of the felted jumper (to give your mittens a nice ribbed cuff) and pin in place. Position the thumb template on the jumper and pin in place. Cut out the fabric pieces by cutting around the templates. Flip the templates, pin in place and repeat to cut out felt pieces for the other hand.

**2** Fold a thumb piece in half with the right side of the fabric facing inwards, so that the corners (shown on the left and right sides of the template) meet. Hand sew from the corners to the top of the thumb (with the 2 adjacent curves) in blanket stitch or running stitch, working close to the edges of the fabric. Ensure that, when you sew the second thumb, it is the mirror image of the first.

**3** Position the left thumb piece on the left-hand piece. It is best to put the thumb piece on your thumb, put the hand piece on your hand and push your thumb through the hole in the hand piece to get a good idea of how to position the thumb piece on the hand piece. Sew the thumb piece in place as before, with the right sides of the fabric facing each other. Repeat with the right hand and thumb pieces.

**4** Fold each mitten in half and sew along the outer edge to complete the glove. Turn the right sides out, and your mittens are ready to wear!

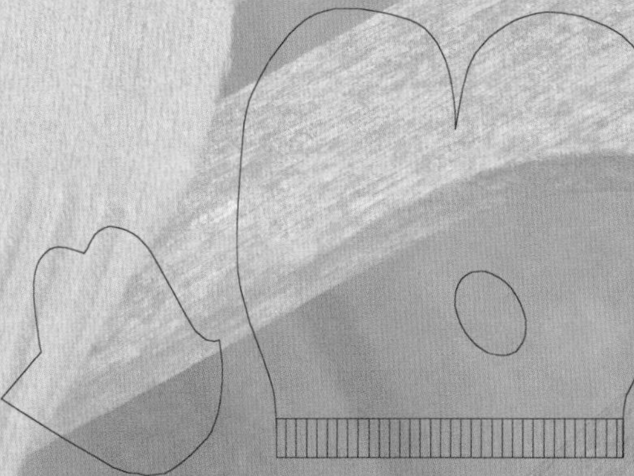

# How to Make
# Bonfire Night Rockets

Finding quirky Bonfire Night decorations is a challenge for even the most trained eye. Yes, it's about the fireworks but, let's face it, once your dad or boyfriend lights a few rockets and fountains, and everyone oohs and ahhs and shouts "be careful", it's all about the food, the décor and being with good friends! These homemade rockets look great, can be put into any vessel and take as long to make as it takes my dad to burn the sausages.

## YOU WILL NEED

✄ plain paper ✄ access to a computer and printer ✄ paper scissors
✄ several cardboard toilet roll tubes (1 tube per rocket) ✄ glue gun and
glue stick ✄ compass ✄ selection of A4 coloured card ✄ hack saw
✄ 2m (6½ft) of 3mm- (⅛in-) wide wooden dowelling

1 To start making your rockets, you will need to find suitable designs to use for the labels. You'll easily find vintage designs by searching online. Once you have found some you like, print out a selection. If they are not the right size, you will need to cut them down – an ordinary cardboard toilet roll tube will need a 9.5cm × 15cm (3¾in × 6in) label.

2 Wrap 1 label around each cardboard tube. Glue it in place with a glue stick.

3 Use a compass to draw circles with a 10cm (4in) diameter (1 for each rocket) on the coloured card. Cut them all out.

4 Take a circle and make a snip from the edge to the centre, then pull 1 newly cut edge across the other to overlap them and form a cone shape. Secure the overlap in place with glue, then repeat with all the circles.

5 Now you need to use the glue gun to stick a cone to the top of each cardboard tube, choosing a colour that complements each label.

6 Next, use the hacksaw to cut your dowelling into pieces of various lengths. Finally, put a blob of glue on the end of each piece of dowelling and attach it to the inside of each cardboard tube, positioning it high enough inside the tube to ensure the glue won't show. Your rockets are now ready to brighten up your garden on Bonfire Night!

# HOW TO CREATE
# THE FIRECRACKER

When it's cold outside but you still want to channel a chic and stylish look at your Guy Fawkes party, try my version of "hat-hair". The Firecracker is a sure-fire way of feeling good with sparkle while ensuring you keep warm. Who says you have to choose comfort over style? I've chosen a beret, but this style is adaptable for other headwear choices.

## YOU WILL NEED

✎ hair mousse ✎ tail comb ✎ curling tongs ✎ curl clips ✎ bristle brush ✎ beret ✎ hairpins and Kirby grips

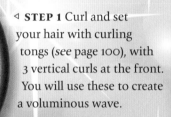

◁ **STEP 1** Curl and set your hair with curling tongs (*see* page 100), with 3 vertical curls at the front. You will use these to create a voluminous wave.

◁ **STEP 2** Once the curls have cooled, take out all the clips except the 3 at the front and lightly brush your hair.

◁ **STEP 3** Add the beret, tilted at an angle and pulled slightly lower on the side of your parting. On this side, form pin curls with the hair that is seen peeking from beneath the hat and use hairpins and grips to secure.

▷ **STEP 4** Leave the curls loose on the other side. If you have longer hair, pin the length underneath while keeping the curls in place at the top, creating a faux bob. Remove the clips from the front 3 curls and gently brush them out into a soft, sweeping wave. Either leave this loose, or put the ends of it into the fuller curls at the sides.

25th of December, Christmas –
the day we eat far too much.

Christmas evokes memories of going shopping with my
mum, cooking with my nan, writing to Father Christmas,
cooking for Father Christmas, WAITING for Father Christmas,
opening presents from Father Christmas and each of us eating our
own body-weight in food, until the entire family is in a food coma.
Actually, thinking about it, nothing has changed.

This chapter takes all my family Christmas classics and turns them
into a celebration that can be enjoyed throughout the festivities.

You are
Invited

Thank You

The turkey took time to be crowned Bird of the British Christmas Table. Peacocks and boars were popular until the turkey graced Henry VIII's Christmas. As an affordable and easily bred bird, turkey won its place by being accessible to the masses. If it's good enough for a king, it's good enough for me, especially in this pie.

# Turkey Stew
## with Herb Dumplings

SERVES 6
PREP 25 mins
COOK about 1 hour

**For the dumplings**

175g (6oz) plain flour

½ tsp baking powder

¼ tsp bicarbonate of soda

½ tsp salt

60g (2¼oz) butter, cubed

3 tbsp chopped rosemary, thyme and parsley (optional)

175ml (6fl oz) buttermilk

1 large free-range egg

**For the filling**

60g (2¼oz) butter

50g (1¾oz) plain flour

750ml (1⅓ pints) turkey stock or a combination of stock and leftover gravy

1 tsp dried thyme

1 bay leaf

salt and black pepper

½ tsp freshly grated nutmeg

¼ tsp Worcestershire sauce

650g (1lb 7oz) cooked turkey or chicken, cut into strips

200g (7oz) frozen peas

1 To make the dumplings, combine the flour, baking powder, bicarbonate of soda and salt in a bowl. Add the butter and rub it in with your fingertips until the mixture resembles coarse breadcrumbs. Stir in the herbs, if using. Cover and refrigerate this mixture while you're making the filling.

2 Preheat the oven to 200°C/fan 180°C/gas mark 6.

3 To make the filling, melt the butter over a medium heat in a large, shallow flameproof casserole dish with a lid. Whisk in the flour and cook for 3 minutes, stirring occasionally.

4 Take the pan off the heat and add the stock or stock and gravy, 200ml (⅓ pint) at a time, whisking it in to prevent lumps from forming. Return the mixture to the heat and season with the thyme, bay leaf, salt and pepper, nutmeg and Worcestershire sauce. Simmer the sauce for 15 minutes, then stir in the meat and peas. Return the filling to a simmer.

5 Meanwhile, whisk the buttermilk and egg together and add this to the dry dumpling mixture all in one go. Stir together until evenly moistened. This should be quite a loose mixture.

6 Scoop a tablespoonful of the mixture into a dumpling shape and place this in the casserole dish with the filling. Repeat with the remaining dumpling mixture – you should have about 12 dumplings. Ensure you leave space between them in the casserole, as they will expand to almost double their size during cooking. Put the lid on the dish and bake for 40–45 minutes.

At Christmas, my mum always put an evergreen wreath on our front door. It always felt inviting and, apparently, it signifies the hope we feel with the oncoming spring and the renewed light. I love this edible take on it, partly because it's delicious, but mostly because everyone oohs at the cuteness factor. I won't tell them it took just 20 minutes to make!

# Sausage Roll Wreath

**SERVES 14**

**PREP** 20 mins, plus chilling

**COOK** 20–25 mins

250g (9oz) shop-bought all-butter puff pastry

14 cocktail sausages

1 free-range egg, beaten

**1** Reserving 50g (1¾oz) of the pastry, roll the remaining 200g (7oz) into a 21cm × 24cm (8¼in × 9½in) rectangle. Cut this in half down the middle so that you have 2 sheets that are 21cm × 12cm (8¼in × 4¾in). Now cut these into 14 rectangles that are 3cm × 12cm (1¼in × 4¾in).

**2** Wrap 1 strip of dough around each cocktail sausage. Roll the remaining 50g (1¾oz) dough into a long, thin strip and form a circle on a baking sheet lined with nonstick baking paper. Brush the circle with some of the beaten

egg and place the mini sausage rolls on top of the pastry circle, side by side, so that each sausage roll is just touching the next.

**3** Brush the sausage rolls with the remaining beaten egg, then chill in the refrigerator for 20 minutes.

**4** Preheat the oven to 200°C/fan 180°C/gas mark 6. Remove the baking sheet with the wreath from the refrigerator and bake for 20–25 minutes until golden brown and puffed up. Serve immediately.

I've often wondered how this delicious combination of pudding batter and sausage got its name, but the origin is disputed. The tasty sausages nestling in their crunchy homes must be eaten with onions and sweet apple and, if you want to take the seasonal festivities a step further, add some cinnamon.

# Mini Toad in the Hole
## with Caramelized Red Onions & Apple Sauce

**MAKES 16**

**PREP 25** mins, plus resting

**COOK 1½** hours

**For the caramelized red onions**

1 tbsp olive oil

1 red onion, thinly sliced

50g (1¾oz) caster sugar

2 tbsp red wine vinegar

salt and black pepper

**For the batter**

75g (2¾oz) self-raising flour

1 free-range egg

100ml (3½fl oz) milk

salt and black pepper

1 tsp vegetable oil

16 cocktail sausages

**For the apple sauce**

30g (1oz) butter

1 Cox's apple, peeled, cored and diced

2 tbsp caster sugar

50ml (2fl oz) apple juice

squeeze of lemon

**To garnish**

1 tsp olive oil

16 sage leaves

**1** For the caramelized onions, heat the oil in a pan set over a low heat and soften the onion for about 10 minutes without allowing it to colour.

**2** Stir in the sugar and vinegar. Season and cook gently over a low heat for 45 minutes until the onions turn a lovely dark golden colour (if it looks as if they might catch, add a splash of water). Taste and add a little more sugar or vinegar if needed. Aim for a sweet and tangy flavour. Set aside.

**3** To make the batter, sift the flour into a large bowl and make a well in the centre. Whisk the egg in a small bowl with the milk and add 50ml (2fl oz) water, stirring to combine. Pour this mixture gradually into the well in the flour, whisking until all the flour has been incorporated. Aim for this mixture to have the consistency of smooth double cream – you may not need all the liquid. Season well and leave the batter to rest for 15 minutes.

**4** Preheat the oven to 220°C/fan 200°C/gas mark 7.

**5** Divide the 1 teaspoon vegetable oil between the cups of a 16-cup mini-muffin tin and place in the oven for 5 minutes until the oil is smoking hot.

**6** Place a cocktail sausage in each muffin cup, then divide the batter between the muffin cups. Bake for 20–25 minutes until the batter has puffed up and is golden.

**7** Meanwhile, for the apple sauce, heat a large frying pan over a medium heat and add the butter. When the butter has melted and is starting to foam, add the apple and sugar. Cook over a medium heat for 5 minutes or until the edges of the apple pieces start to brown. Add the apple and lemon juices and cook over a medium heat until the apples are golden brown and the sauce has thickened.

**8** For the garnish, heat the oil in a small frying pan. Fry the sage leaves for 10 seconds each until just crisp.

**9** Turn out the toads and arrange them on serving plates or a tray. Spoon a dollop of the apple sauce into the centre of each pudding, then finish each with caramelized onions and a crisp-fried sage leaf.

Why do supermarkets go crazy packaging cheese selections at Christmas time? Because this time of year is all about indulgence, and I do like to indulge in a cheese board with a glass of port. But I choose the cheeses I like and, as ever, I love to add my own twist. Family and friends always giggle at me when I make "Cheesy Presents" – I know most of them wouldn't have the patience. But these delights rate too highly on cuteness charts to be left out!

# CHEESY PRESENTS

**MAKES 1**

**PREP 20 mins,**
plus chilling

1 tsp finely chopped fresh dill or ½ tsp dried dill

¼ tsp garlic powder

1 red pepper, half finely diced, half reserved for decoration

1 spring onion, the white finely diced, the green reserved for garnish

salt and black pepper

300g (10½oz) cream cheese

a selection of crackers, to serve

**1** Mix the dill, garlic powder, diced red pepper, diced white spring onion and salt and pepper to taste into the cream cheese.

**2** Line the tub that the cream cheese came in with clingfilm, then pack the cream-cheese mixture back into the tub.

**3** Refrigerate the cheese until 20 minutes before you are ready to serve, then place the tub in the freezer for 20 minutes to firm up and to ensure that it holds its shape.

**4** To make the garnish, cut the reserved red pepper into small dice and 1 rectangular shape (the gift tag). Next, choose a firm section from the green part of the spring onion, cut off about 5cm (2in) and make incisions lengthways from the bottom of the onion to two-thirds of the way up. Place it in a bowl of iced water and the spring onion should open up like a bow or a flower. Choose a few nice long green pieces and blanch them in hot water for about 10 seconds, then quench in cold water and dry. This will soften the onion and you can then use it as the string for the present.

**5** Before serving, set the unwrapped block of cheese on a platter. Decorate it with the spring onion leaves and bow and the red pepper squares and gift tag, and serve with crackers.

Although the florentine is Italian in origin, my family adopted it as if it was their natural-born child. Crunchy, fruity, nutty, chocolatey – yummy! We made them as gifts and used dark, white and milk chocolate to cover them. However, more often than not, they never made it out of the kitchen!

# ANGELIC STAR FLORENTINES

**MAKES 16**

**PREP** 20 mins, plus chilling, cooling and setting

**COOK** 20–25 mins

30g (1oz) glacé cherries

100g (3½oz) flaked almonds

30g (1oz) raisins

50g (1¾oz) candied peel

30g (1oz) candied angelica

50g (1¾oz) butter

50g (1¾oz) caster sugar

50g (1¾oz) plain flour

2 tsp golden syrup

2 tsp double cream

100–150g (3½–5½oz) milk chocolate

**1** Line 2 large baking sheets with nonstick baking paper. Chop the cherries into quarters, then mix them with the almonds, raisins, candied peel and angelica in a bowl.

**2** Melt the butter with the sugar and flour in a small saucepan set over a very low heat, stirring continuously. Once the butter has melted and the flour and sugar are fully mixed in, add the syrup and stir through.

**3** Remove the mixture from the heat and stir in the cream. You should end up with a very thick, homogenous liquid. Add the almonds and fruit and mix thoroughly.

**4** Place a star-shaped cookie cutter on a prepared baking sheet. Divide the mixture into 16 equal-sized portions. Take a portion and press it into the star-shaped cutter. Repeat with the remaining mixture, using the cutter to shape the mixture into star shapes. Place the baking sheets in the freezer for 20 minutes. Preheat the oven to 180°C/fan 160°C/gas mark 4.

**5** Bake for 10–12 minutes until the biscuits are golden brown. Remove from the oven, leave to cool on the baking sheet, then transfer to a wire rack to finish cooling.

**6** Break the chocolate into pieces and melt it in a heatproof bowl set over a saucepan of barely simmering water, ensuring the base of the bowl doesn't touch the water below. Spoon a little chocolate onto the flat side of each florentine, spread it across the biscuit, then leave for about 30 minutes to harden.

Friends, family, colleagues and clients... the list of people I want to show thanks to at Christmas seems endless. These biscuits make a perfect gift, especially if you can get your hands on a few vintage Christmas tins to present them in!

# PINWHEEL COOKIES

**MAKES** 30
**PREP** 25 mins, plus chilling
**COOK** 10–12 mins

250g (9oz) unsalted butter, softened

100g (3½oz) caster sugar

1 tsp vanilla extract

¼ tsp salt

250g (9oz) plain flour, sifted, plus extra for dusting

3 tbsp cocoa powder

**1** Cream the butter and sugar together with a wooden spoon or an electric whisk until light and fluffy. Gently fold in the vanilla extract and salt. Gradually fold in the flour to form a loose, crumbly dough.

**2** Turn out the dough on a lightly floured work surface and knead it for 1–2 minutes by pushing small amounts of it away from you with the heel of your hand. Divide the dough in half. Sprinkle the cocoa powder over 1 of the halves, then knead until it has been fully incorporated. Cover the 2 balls of dough with clingfilm and chill in the refrigerator for 1 hour.

**3** Remove the dough from the refrigerator and roll out each piece on a sheet of lightly floured clingfilm to a 16cm × 25cm (6¼in × 10in) rectangle. Invert the chocolate dough onto the plain dough. Remove the clingfilm and press the doughs firmly together. Now roll up the stack as though it were a roulade, rolling from a long edge. Cover the log and chill for 30 minutes.

**4** Preheat the oven to 180°C/fan 160°C/gas mark 4. Line a baking sheet with nonstick baking paper. Using a very sharp knife, cut the log into 30 × 5mm (¼in) slices. Put these on the prepared baking sheet and bake for 10–12 minutes. Allow the biscuits to cool on the baking sheet for a couple of minutes before gently placing on a wire rack to cool completely.

If you really want to show off, make up some of these chequer cookies. They are a little bit fiddly, but Christmas is all about giving, and the lucky recipient will taste your hard work 100 per cent!

# CHEQUER COOKIES

MAKES 30

PREP 35 mins, plus chilling

COOK 10–12 mins

250g (9oz) unsalted butter, softened

100g (3½oz) caster sugar

1 tsp vanilla extract

¼ tsp salt

250g (9oz) plain flour, sifted, plus extra for dusting

3 tbsp cocoa powder

1 large free-range egg

1 Cream the butter and sugar together with a wooden spoon or an electric whisk until light and fluffy. Fold in the vanilla extract and salt. Gradually fold in the flour to form a loose, crumbly dough.

2 Turn out the dough on a lightly floured work surface and knead it for 1–2 minutes. Divide the dough in half. Sprinkle the cocoa powder over 1 of the halves, then knead until it has been fully incorporated. Cover the 2 balls of dough with clingfilm and chill in the refrigerator for 1 hour.

3 Remove the dough from the refrigerator and place each piece of dough between 2 sheets of clingfilm. Using a rolling pin, roll each piece of dough into a 7.5cm × 15cm (3in × 6in) rectangle that's about 1cm (½in) thick. Using a sharp knife and a ruler, slice each rectangle into 5 × 1.5cm- (⅝in-) wide strips.

4 Whisk the egg with 1 tablespoon water. Put a sheet of clingfilm on your work surface. Put 3 dough strips on it, alternating between white and brown strips. Brush the tops and between the strips with egg wash, then press the strips together. Repeat, stacking 3 strips above the first to form second and third layers, alternating colours in a chequerboard effect. You will be left with 1 dough strip; roll this out thinly and wrap it around the log. Wrap the log in clingfilm. Chill for 30 minutes in the refrigerator or for 15 minutes in the freezer.

5 Preheat the oven to 180°C/fan 160°C/gas mark 4. Line a baking sheet with nonstick baking paper. Slice each log into 15 × 5mm (¼in) slices and place the cookies on the prepared baking sheet. Bake for 10–12 minutes, then leave to cool for 2 minutes before transferring to a wire rack to cool completely.

These soft, gooey truffles are gloriously festive. Truffles are orthodox at all our family events, and Christmas allows us to go boozy with them. My festive list includes orange liqueur, Irish cream, brandy and whisky, and if you are feeling really lazy, the supermarkets sell creams with them in, so you just add chocolate! Ho ho ho! Yum Yum Yum.

# SNOWMEN RUM & CHOCOLATE TRUFFLES

MAKES 6
PREP 30 mins,
plus chilling
CHILL 1–1½ hours

150ml (¼ pint) double cream

knob of unsalted butter

150g (5½oz) good-quality dark chocolate (with at least 70 per cent cocoa solids), broken into small pieces

pinch of sea salt

1 tbsp rum, or to taste

200g (7oz) desiccated coconut

50g (1¾oz) marzipan

few drops of orange food colouring

24 raisins

1 Heat the cream in a saucepan set over a medium heat until nearly boiling. As soon as tiny bubbles start to appear, add the butter. When it has melted, pour the mixture over the chocolate pieces in a bowl, whisking as you go, so that the chocolate melts slowly. Add the salt and the rum to the mixture.

2 Once the chocolate has melted and the mixture is smooth, pour it into a glass bowl and chill in the refrigerator for 1 hour until it is firm enough to shape, but not too solid.

3 Scatter the desiccated coconut over a large, clean work surface. Using a teaspoon, take a scoop of chocolate from the bowl and shape it into a ball using your

palms, then roll the ball in the coconut until covered. Continue until you have 18 balls. To assemble the snowmen's bodies, skewer 1 ball with a cocktail stick, then repeat with 2 more to make a stack of 3 balls. Repeat with the remaining balls until you have 6 snowmen.

4 To make the noses, combine the marzipan with orange food colouring. Shape the marzipan into 6 little hook-shaped noses, then press these onto the snowmen's faces. Use 2 raisins for eyes, and 2 for buttons on each snowman. Put the snowmen on a baking sheet, plate or tray and chill in the refrigerator for at least 30 minutes. Remove 30 minutes before serving.

Christmas would not be complete without a sweet made with dried fruits and spices. Christmas cake started out as plum porridge to line the stomach after a day of fasting and evolved over time into today's version, apparently with the help of wise men that brought over exciting Eastern spices. My nan's a wise old woman, so I stole her recipe!

**SERVES 14**

**PREP** 40 mins, plus soaking and cooling

**COOK** 2¾ hours

# CHRISTMAS BALL

200g (7oz) glacé cherries

300g (10½oz) currants

100g (3½oz) dried pineapple

100g (3½oz) raisins

200g (7oz) candied peel

250ml (9fl oz) dry red wine

125g (4½oz) butter, softened, plus extra for greasing

175g (6oz) caster sugar

4 free-range eggs

200ml (⅓ pint) black treacle

1 tsp bicarbonate of soda

2 tsp ground cinnamon

½ tsp ground cloves

½ tsp ground nutmeg

1 tsp vanilla extract

200g (7oz) chopped walnuts

450g (1lb) plain flour, sifted

**To decorate**

100g (3½oz) butter, softened

100g (3½oz) icing sugar

grated rind of 1 orange

6 kumquats, thinly sliced

150g (5½oz) caster sugar

about 250g (9oz) Christmas berries (we used redcurrants)

**1** In a large bowl, soak the candied and dried fruits and peel in the wine for 1 hour. Preheat the oven to 150°C/fan 130°C/gas mark 2. Grease the 2 halves of a 15cm (6in) spherical cake mould.

**2** Cream the butter and sugar together with a wooden spoon or an electric whisk until light and fluffy, then gradually stir in the eggs. Beat until smooth, then set aside. In small bowl, combine the black treacle and bicarbonate of soda and beat this into the butter mixture. Add the cinnamon, cloves, nutmeg and vanilla extract. Mix well with a large wooden spoon, then set the mixture aside.

**3** In small bowl, combine the walnuts with 1 tablespoon of the flour. Stir these into the fruit-and-wine mixture until well combined. Add to the butter-and-spice mixture and mix well.

**4** Gradually stir in the remaining flour. Divide the mixture between the 2 halves of the prepared cake mould and bake for 15 minutes. Continue baking at 130°C/fan 110°C/gas mark ¾ for 2¼ hours until a skewer inserted into the cake comes out clean. Leave the cake to stand for 10 minutes, then remove it from the tin and let it cool on a wire rack. Once it is cool, cut it in half horizontally into 2 layers.

**5** To make the decoration, combine the softened butter and icing sugar until smooth. Mix in the orange rind and set aside. Place the sliced kumquats in a saucepan with the caster sugar and 100ml (3½fl oz) water and cook over a low heat until they are lightly caramelized and the liquid is syrupy.

**6** To assemble, spread the butter icing between the 2 layers of the cake and sandwich together. Place the kumquats on the cake over the icing and brush the entire cake with the kumquat cooking syrup. Decorate the base and top with Christmas berries.

Eggnog was as much a part of our family Christmas as, let's say, our cat. In my earliest memories, my brother and I are knocking it back to our hearts' content (I'm pretty sure now that my dad must have reduced the alcohol content). Although it's easy to buy eggnog ready-made, the extra effort is well worth it for a lighter, tastier, tantalizing creamy explosion!

# WHITE CHRISTMAS EGGNOG

**SERVES 6**

**PREP 10** mins, plus cooling and chilling

**COOK 10** mins

4 large free-range eggs

2 large free-range egg yolks

100g (3½oz) granulated sugar

600ml (1 pint) whole milk

½ tbsp vanilla extract

175ml (6fl oz) golden rum

125ml (4fl oz) 80 per cent proof bourbon

¼ tsp freshly grated nutmeg, plus extra to decorate

200ml (⅓ pint) whipping cream

1 tbsp icing sugar

redcurrants, to decorate

**1** In a large bowl, whisk together the eggs, egg yolks and granulated sugar until smooth. Pour the mixture into a large heavy-based saucepan. Gradually stir in the milk, blending well. Heat the mixture slowly over a very low heat, stirring continuously until it reaches 71–77°C (160–170°F) on a jam or sugar thermometer. If you don't have a jam or sugar thermometer, you should cook the custard until it is thick enough to coat the back of a spoon (if you draw your finger across the custard on the back of the spoon, the line you make should remain distinct).

**2** Pour the custard through a fine-meshed sieve into a large bowl. Stir in the vanilla extract, rum, bourbon and nutmeg. Leave the mixture to cool, then cover with clingfilm and refrigerate for at least 3 hours or for up to 1 day until cold.

**3** Just before serving, whip the cream to very soft peaks, beating in the icing sugar as you go. Gently fold the cream into the custard mixture until incorporated.

**4** Pour the eggnog into glasses and decorate with a little grated nutmeg and redcurrants.

This delicious hot spiced tea screams "drink me!" It celebrates all the amazing flavours we expect to taste at Christmas and provides a fantastic light alternative and accompaniment to everything. I love to serve it up in jars topped with my homemade Christmas Toppers (see page 151) with spices and fruits on show in the jar to elevate the taste buds and provide visual delight!

# Hot Spiced Tea

SERVES 6

PREP 5 mins, plus steeping

COOK 10 mins

1 cinnamon stick

6 allspice berries

3 cloves

4 tea bags

100g (3½oz) demerara sugar

140ml (4½fl oz) cranberry juice

60ml (2¼fl oz) orange juice

1 tbsp lemon juice

6 tbsp cranberries

**1** Place the cinnamon stick, allspice and cloves on a double thickness of muslin. Bring up the corners of the cloth and tie them with a length of string to form a bag around the spices.

**2** Place 1 litre (1¾ pints) water and the spice bag in a large saucepan and bring to the boil. Take the pan off the heat and add the tea bags. Cover the pan and leave the mixture to steep for 5 minutes. Discard the tea and spice bags. Stir in the sugar until dissolved. Add the juices and heat through. Place 1 tablespoon of the cranberries into each of 6 jars and pour over the hot tea. Serve immediately.

Bucket Bunting

# HOW TO MAKE
# BUCKET BUNTING

This decoration will need a bit of time investment at the start, but can be used every year. You can put anything you want in the cute little buckets, covering the contents with some scrunched-up gold tissue paper to keep it a surprise.

## YOU WILL NEED

✀ access to a photocopier, computer and printer ✀ paper scissors ✀ 24 mini tin buckets

✀ 24 chosen images for buckets ✀ 25 sheets plain A4 paper ✀ pencil ✀ glue gun

✀ 1.5m (5ft) metal link chain (available in DIY stores) ✀ 24 large jump rings (8mm/³⁄₈in or larger)

✀ flat-nosed pliers ✀ treats of your choice

1 To make decorative covers for the buckets, photocopy and cut out the template opposite and wrap it around a bucket to check it for size. Resize it as necessary to fit your buckets. Find images you like online and print them on plain paper at sizes that work with your template. Place your template on top of the printed image, draw around the template and cut the bucket cover out. Taking 1 cover, bend it around a bucket, gluing as you go with a glue gun.

2 For advent-calendar bunting, photocopy and cut out the numbered labels on the opposite page and stick them to your buckets as shown in the picture. For a nice neat finish to your buckets, cut out 3mm- (¹⁄₈in-) wide strips of coloured card and glue 1 around the base of each bucket. Allow the glue to dry.

3 Now attach the buckets to the chain. If your chain is 1.5m (5ft) long, space the buckets about 6cm (2½in) apart. (For chains of a different length, divide the length by 24 to establish the spacing.) Bend each jump ring open and shut with pliers, joining a link of chain and a bucket handle each time. Now hang your bunting over the fireplace or around the tree and fill with treats of your choice.

DAY 1

DAY 7

DAY 13

DAY 19

DAY 2

DAY 8

DAY 14

DAY 20

DAY 3

DAY 9

DAY 15

DAY 21

DAY 4

DAY 10

DAY 16

DAY 22

DAY 5

DAY 11

DAY 17

DAY 23

DAY 6

DAY 12

DAY 18

DAY 24

BUCKET COVER
TEMPLATE

# HOW TO CREATE a
# SEQUIN SNOOD

Christmas is the time to go for full-on Hollywood glamour with your hair, and if you're looking for a practical fuss-free hairstyle that still looks beautiful, let us introduce you to the snood! This nifty headgear has been around since medieval times and was very popular in the 40s. It is half cap, half hairnet, is usually pinned at the top of the crown, gathering the length of the hair, and works wonders when you haven't time to do the back of your hair. Just a few customizations can transform it into an eye-catching hair accessory that exudes vintage glamour. The snood can be dressed up or down. Try adding sequins, flowers, ribbons – whatever you like. Make it truly festive with shades of red, gold and green. Styling the front of your hair into victory rolls or elaborate curls will take it from daytime to glam eveningwear.

## YOU WILL NEED

❧ hair mousse ❧ tail comb ❧ heated rollers ❧ section clips ❧ bristle brush ❧ hair grips and hairpins ❧ snood (slumbernet) of your choice (available in pharmacies) ❧ hairspray

△ **STEP 1** Curl and set your hair in heated rollers. This style needs a lot of volume at the front, so start applying the rollers at the hairline and work your way backwards (rather than working downwards in horizontal sections). Leave the rollers in while your hair cools.

△ **STEP 2** Take out the back rollers and section this area off with clips while you work on the front.

△ **STEP 3** Remove the rollers from the front of the hair and divide this into 3 sections by parting your hair above each eyebrow. Gently backcomb the side sections, then smooth with a bristle brush and create a victory roll (*see page 220–21*) on each side.

◁ **STEP 4** Add the snood, pinning it at the crown using hair grips as close to your own hair colour as possible. Turn your attention to the front section. To make a curled quiff, sweep the curls back off the face with your hands and pin in place. (The rollers would have created the volume needed to do this.) Spray liberally with hairspray.

# VINTAGE PATISSERIE THANK YOU ♥

**93 Feet East**  For allowing me to host my parties at your amazing venue, which allowed me to grow my business! *www.93feeteast.co.uk*

**Ariotek**  For being the best web-hosting company I've ever come across. Drew and Collin, you are both amazing! *ariotek.co.uk*

**Barnett Lawson Trimmings**  For being the only haberdashery I'll ever need. London is worth a visit just for you. *www.bltrimmings.com*

**Beauty Seen PR**  Michelle, you are an amazing businesswoman. Thank you for supporting us, both as a client, and as a REVLON sponsor! We adore you! *www.beautyseenpr.com*

**Benefit Cosmetics**  For making the Big Beautiful Eyes product. *www.benefitcosmetics.com*

**Benjamin Spriggs**  Thank you for your support and for always thinking of me! *www.thesundaytimes.co.uk/sto/public/style/?CMP=KNGvccp1-style+magazine*

**Bethan Soanes**  For being stunning and being there for The Vintage Patisserie everytime we need you! *www.bethan-soanes.co.uk*

**Beyond Retro**  For being a one-stop shop for all things vintage, and for being the place from which most of my wardrobe originates! *www.beyondretro.com*

**Carolyn Whitehorne**  For support, encouragement and advice. *www.toniandguy.com*

**Cass Stainton**  For getting me, and for throwing some pretty amazing parties!

**Cate at Bitch Buzz**  Darlin', I love your energy, ambition, drive and humour – I'm a FAN! *www.bitchbuzz.com*

**Charlotte Grace Figg**  Thank you for being part of the team and always bringing new energy every time I see you. I always smile when I am in your company. *www.thefollymixtures.co.uk*

**Ciara Kate Callaghan**  For having amazing energy, for doing some writing and research for book one and for being the cutest thing ever!

**Cliff Fluet**  For becoming my friend, for support, for encouragement and for understanding what I want to achieve. Cliff, you are amazing. *www.lewissilkin.com*

**Company Magazine**  For support, always. *www.company.co.uk*

**Dandy Dan**  You are a true gentleman. I know you work in-house now, but I still want that coffee we talked about!

**David Carter**  For being a loyal eccentric dandy. Your creativeness has no limits. P.S. I think I did sell more books than you, no? :-) *www.alacarter.com*

**Deborah Meaden**  For believing in me and providing me with a stepping stone to grow my business. It's been lovely seeing you this year and I always feel so proud when telling you about my achievements. Thank you. *www.deborahmeaden.com*

**Denise Bates**  For being so supportive, incredibly fair and proud!

**Denhams Broadcast & Digital**  To Jill (for being a little mental) and Grace. For believing. *www.denhams.tv*

**Eleanor Maxfield**  For commissioning the first book and for totally getting the second book! For being by my side and supporting me every step of the way. You believe, you care and you are always fair. That totally rhymes! So happy you have become my friend. It's been beyond amazing.

**Elnett Hairspray**  What would we do without you? *www.loreal-paris.co.uk/styling/elnett.aspx*

**Emma Perris**  For the wonderful massages you give, for support and for being my mate! *emmaperris.co.uk*

**Fleur Britten**  For being fabulous and supportive. It was lovely to see you as a beautiful mum! *www.fleurbritten.moonfruit.com*

**Fleur de Guerre**  For being a gorgeous and talented lady. For jumping in when I have needed you, and for being a good friend. Please stop being so fabulous! *www.diaryofavintagegirl.com*

**Fraser Doherty and Anthony McGinley**  For being business inspirations; I'm always so proud to say you are my friends! *www.superjam.co.uk*

**Grazia**  For support. *www.graziadaily.co.uk*

**Harper's Bazaar**  For support. *www.harpersbazaar.com*

**Hazel Holtham**  For being an amazing businesswoman and friend. Hazel, you are a beauty inside and out and it's been a joy watching your business develop, and even more of a joy to watch you fall in love! *www.ragandbow.com*

**John Moore**  For training me when I was 18, for helping at every step of the way, for caring and being a true friend. *www.rsmtenon.com*

**Karen Baker**  For creating a wealth of press that only a person who cares and is driven could achieve! You do the work of a team and I could not ask for more. Thank you for being so wonderful. It's been lovely seeing you fall in love and your eyes twinkle!

**Kathy at Past Perfect**  For having a brilliant company that sells amazing music! *www.pastperfect.com*

**Katie, Poppy and Richard**  For being the first to make a real business out of vintage. You are the leader OH KATIE! For being my friend and inspiring me. Thanks for supporting. Lets take over the world ;-) *www.whatkatiedid.com*

**Lady Luck (AKA El Nino and Tomoko)**  For being the first Vintage Dance Club in London and both being so fabulous. *www.ladyluckclub.co.uk*

**Laura Fyfe and Maura Cook**  Laura, you're talented, hard-working and a really nice and fair person. I could not have asked for a better home economist. You totally got the project and I hope I get to work with you again. Maura, thank you for your amazing energy and for being such a great spirit to have around. Laura is lucky to have you as a sidekick! *laurafyfe.tumblr.com*

**Laura Cherry**  For being such a beauty, inside and out. You are an inspiring, hard-working lady and I'm proud that you are achieving your dream. Thank you for being part of the team.

**Lauren Craig**  For caring about where your flowers come from, for being so talented and for being my friend. *www.thinkingflowers.org.uk*

**Lauren Mittell**  For continued hard work and support! You have allowed this year to happen for me. You're gorgeous inside and out and I look forward to seeing you achieve your dreams.

**Leanne Bryan**  Thank you for caring and being so gentle and calming. I could not ask for more from an editor! I missed all your questions on this book asking me what this and that meant! That either means I'm getting better at writing, or you understand my weirdness more!

**Lian Hirst**  For having the best Fashion PR label in town. Thank you for understanding and supporting and being an amazing friend. I can't tell you how proud I am of what you have achieved! *www.tracepublicity.com*

**Linton at The Fox**  For allowing me to host my parties at The Fox, which helped me to grow my business. And for nothing ever being any trouble; Linton, you are amazing. *www.thefoxpublichouse.co.uk*

**Lipstick & Curls**  For your inspiring hairstyles and for being amazingly talented. *www.lipstickandcurls.net*

**Louis Roederer Champagne**  James, I would like to thank you for making the launch of our first book so special. Thank you for believing in the brand and allowing us to have copius amounts of the best Champagne we have ever tasted (and that was unamimous!). *www.champagne-roederer.com/en/*

**M·A·C Cosmetics**  For creating the perfect look. What would a girl do without her Ruby Woo! *www.maccosmetics.com/index.tmpl*

**Margaret at Vintage Heaven**  Margaret! You are the most amazing woman that roams the planet! Your positivity fills my heart. Thank you for having the most fabulous business and for filling in the gaps in the book. I truly love you! In fact I want to be you! *vintageheaven.co.uk*

**Mehmet at Can Supermarket**  Thank you for everything!

**Naomi and Vintage Secrets**  For your support and for your love of all things vintage. *www.vintagesecret.com*

**Nina Butkovich-Budden**  Oh Nina! Leader of the vintage hair pack! You are so talented, I could watch you work for hours. Thank you for styling the hair for the New Year chapter. A.M.A.Z.I.N.G! *www.ninashairparlour.com*

**Octopus Publishing Group team**  For all being so lovely and for believing in this book! *www.octopusbooks.co.uk*

**Patrick at Value My Stuff**  For being inspiring and having such a great business. *www.valuemystuff.com*

**Peter and Sasha**  For always bringing amazing life to every party! I wish I could have you more!

**Pete Katsiaounis**  For doing the illustrations for all my websites. You go beyond the call of duty. *www.inkandmanners.com*

**Rob Davies**  For having an amazing business and being a friend. Your energy and support always make me smile. Thank you. *www.tracepublicity.com*

**Rokit**  Thank you for being the first vintage shop I ever bought anything in! Imogen Excell, they are lucky to have you. *www.rokit.co.uk*

**Rosie Alia Johnson**  For being a beautiful spirit and part of the team, for bringing the first clothes collection to life! You are a very talented beauty. *www.rosiealia.blogspot.co.uk*

**Sales at Octopus Publishing Group**  Becs, Kevin, Siobhan, Terry, Vanessa… Sales! Thank you for getting the book out into the big wide world! You do me proud and I know you talk about the book with passion. Thank you!

**Sarah Keen**  For being so bloody "ON IT". I love working with you, and having you as my crafty Girl Friday on this book was amazing. You did a stunning job. Thank you.

**Sharon Trickett** For being incredibly hard-working and talented and utterly fabulous. It's been lovely watching you grow Minnie Moons. *www.minniemoons.com*

**Simone Hadfield** Thank you for your hard work and kindness always… Not to mention your beauty! *www.miss-turnstiles.blogspot.co.uk*

**Sophia Hunt, Belladonna Beauty Parlour** Thank you for creating the fabulous hairstyles throughout this book. I'm so proud and happy you were part of the team. You are an incredibly talented lady and I wish you luck in whatever your future holds.

**Sophie Laurimore** For being a very supportive agent and for understanding my life. It's been great growing our businesses together. Thanks to you and your family for being in my Christmas chapter! *www.factualmanagement.com*

**Stylist** For support. *www.stylist.co.uk*

**Susie and the Luna & Curious team** Susie, your creativity inspires me. You must see this in everything I do now. Thank you for bringing the Luna & Curious people together and for your 24/7 support! *www.lunaandcurious.blogspot.com*

**Time Out London** For continued support. *www.timeout.com/london*

**Top Shelf Jazz** Always there to perform a treat! Thank you for always being amazing at everything I have booked you for. *www.topshelfjazz.com*

**Uncle Roy's** For selling edible flowers (roses) and having the most fabulous company. *www.uncleroys.co.uk*

**Wella Hair** For making the best hair products. *www.wella.com*

**Yasia Williams-Leedham** For so much I don't know where to begin. Firstly, for your dedication and hard work. For your love of this project. For understanding what I want in your sleep! I don't think I could work with anyone else (well, I wouldn't want to, for sure!). I love you YW!

**Yuki Sugiura** For caring and for being so talented and creative. Work is not meant to be this much fun! You understand exactly how my mind works and together we are a great team. Your food photography makes me smile like a Cheshire cat. *www.yukisugiura.com*

**Zippos Circus** Thank you for lending us your fabulous circus equipment. You brought the children's tea party to life! When I visited your headquarters, it was one of the most special days I've had in a long time. Not only are you an incredibly amazing circus but your academy and library were breathtaking. I love that you are not precious about the amazing props you hire out to make people's parties special. Thank you for letting me into your world. *www.zipposcircus.co.uk*

# Angel Adoree THANK you

**Adele Mildred** Thank you darlin' for being an inspiring creative beauty. I'm lucky to have you illustrate the book and thank you for caring that it's perfect. You are a darlin' friend and I can't wait to celebrate your wedding with you!

**Alison Coward** Thank you for being so proud and supporting me every step of the way.

**Andreya Triana** It's been a joy seeing you fall in love this year! Thank you for filling my life with music and love and endless praise! If I could sing I'd ask for a voice like yours.

**Bobby Nicholls and Lord Ian** You will always be my best party boys… I just need to party more! Please can we make this happen? Bobby, I love you! It's been amazing watching you grow into the King of Creatives!

**Christina Lau** I always feel very emotional when I need to express my thank yous to you. Thank you for your love and continued belief in me, for teaching me how to bake, and for helping with websites and business problems. You are my friend and my mentor, and one of the few people I can turn to for help. I love you darlin'.

**Darren Whelan** My oldest friend. Thank you for your love and support, and for reminding me to stop every now and again! Congratulations on your new life! I'm so happy for you. You and Kelly will be the best parents to your princess Nahla.

**David Edwards** You are my dearest friend, the perfect gentleman and a creative wizard. Your bread-making is a bit ropey, but none of us are perfect :-). Thank you for your endless support and stunning photography. I love you! And I can't wait to celebrate your wedding with you!

**Dick Stawbridge** I fell in love with you because you make me so happy. You make me laugh (often with bad humour), you care more than anyone I have ever met, you give so much and you inspire me with your energy, positivity and intelligence but, most importantly, with your pork-belly-making skills.

**Elizabeth Osbourne** Thank you for caring and teaching me to read. Your memory has never been forgotten.

**Fred and Katja Künzi** For taking me out of London and giving me the best memories I could wish for.

**Gaia Facchini (Mouthful O' Jam)** You slipped into our lives and it's like you were always here. Thank you.

**Gary Nurse** What a pleasure it's been seeing you be a sensational father. I'm so proud of you. Thank you for your friendship and support, and for knowing me well enough to always have a right answer in a crisis! Not only are you a handsome gent, but the beauty goes much deeper and I love you so much for this.

**Gossica Anichebe** For making me laugh, and for your love and friendship. Thank you.

**Grandma, Nan and the rest of the ladies in my family** For your constant love and kindness, and for being so proud of my achievements. I love you all.

**Helen Carter** For supporting me and believing in me… and for coming to my rescue!

**Jake Telford and family** For being the best sax player and my favourite ginger. Thank you.

**Jim Walker** For living at the end of garden! For being my dearest friend. For your love and support, and for your proudness. I love you.

**John, Julie and Katie Walker** My second family! Thank you for the love you send me from all the way over the pond… Not to mention for taking me around all the vintage shops every time I came to visit!

**Joseph Yianna** For your friendship and support, and for being so fabulous!

**Judith Biffiger** For sharing your world, inspiring me with music and love, and being the gentlest, sweetest person ever!

**Karen Pearson** For being a friend and a business inspiration. Essex girls rule!

**Kate and Joe Skully** For making me laugh until my sides split, for being bloody fabulous and for the love and support you have always shown me. Kate, it was lots of fun staging your hen party!

**Leah Prentice** For being the second Vintage Patisserie team member. And for being my mate and causing me to laugh too many times. Mwah!

**LeaLea Jones** For singing like an angel, for your open heart, for knowing that hard work pays off. Ms Jones, you are an inspiration to me and your peers around you. Hackney is a lucky place.

**Lee and Fiona Behan** Life's a pitch and I'll never forget it! Thank you for inspiring and supporting me!

**Leo Chadburn** I'll always remember how we met. I was sitting in a bar with my feet on the table and you approached me and said "Your shoes are fabulous. Would you like to party?" I'm not quite sure if that's how it happened, but that's what I'll go with! Thirteen years of friendship and I love you so much. Your mum was proud of what an amazing son she has.

**Mel Patel** For being my mate and the only DJ I'd ever employ.

**Mum and Dad** For allowing me to be me. For showing me how to be open. For showing me how to love and give unconditionally. I'm the person I am because of you both. I know you tell me how proud you are of me, but I am proud of you both, too.

**Natasha** For your love and support.

**Paul, Grandad and the rest of the men in my family** For the love and kindness you've always shown me. Thank you.

**Sarah, Leroy, Henry and Oscar** The panda dress is getting closer! Thank you for going beyond the call of friendship and believing in me. Sarah, it's lovely to see you being such an amazing mum. I'm so proud you are my mate!

**Seymour Nurse** When I see your name, I smile. Your kind words live in my heart and I'll love you forever, Peter Pan!

**Taj Cambridge** It's been a hell of a year, babes! Every day we take a step closer towards our dream. I love you, I'm so proud of what you have achieved this year and my heart is made warm seeing you smile more than ever.

**Tate and Anthony** You two love birds are so inspiring with your business ventures! I love being around you and learning new stuff! *www.anytodo.com* is genius and that's purely because of you both.

**The Strawbridges** It's worrying that I feel so at home with you because you are all wonderfully crazy! Thank you for making me feel part of the family. I love you all.

**Val and Co at the Palm Tree** For giving me the best nights of my life and for being such a lovely family.

**Vicki, Young, Rosy and Theo** For your love and support, and for the party years! It's been amazing watching you grow as a family and I'm proud to be your friend.

Special thanks go to all the beautiful people who modelled for the book.

A gesture of kindness and support will never go without recognition in my world. Thank you for buying this book, thank you to the companies that have sold my book and thank you for reading my thank yous. I hope that I get to meet you one day and that you see how happy you have made me.

# INDEX

## PICTURE CREDITS

Alamy/Sean Gladwell 36–7 (background). Corbis/Images.com 18 (background). Fotolia/AlessandraM 268 (background); cecile02 128–9 (background); davorr 220–1 (background). Getty Images/Michael Rosenfeld 282 (background).